The Pity of Partition

LAWRENCE STONE LECTURES

Sponsored by
The Shelby Cullom Davis Center for Historical Studies
and Princeton University Press
2011

A list of titles in this series appears
at the back of the book.

AYESHA JALAL

The Pity of Partition

Manto's Life,
Times, and Work
across the
India-Pakistan
Divide

Princeton University Press
Princeton and Oxford

Copyright © 2013 by Princeton University Press
Published by Princeton University Press, 41 William Street,
Princeton, New Jersey 08540
In the United Kingdom: Princeton University Press, 6 Oxford Street,
Woodstock, Oxfordshire OX20 1TW

press.princeton.edu

Jacket photographs: Manto in a pensive mood, Lahore. Courtesy of the Manto archive.
Indian refugees crowd onto trains as a result of the creation of two independent states,
India and Pakistan, 1947, Amritsar, India. © Bettmann/CORBIS

Library of Congress Cataloging-in-Publication Data

Jalal, Ayesha.
    The pity of partition : Manto's life, times, and work across the India-Pakistan divide /
Ayesha Jalal.
        p.   cm. — (Lawrence Stone lectures)
    Includes bibliographical references and index.
    ISBN 978-0-691-15362-9 (hardcover : acid-free paper) 1. Manto, Sa'adat Hasan,
1912–1955—Criticism and interpretation. 2. Manto, Sa'adat Hasan, 1912–1955—Political
and social views. 3. Manto, Sa'adat Hasan, 1912–1955—Correspondence. 4. India—
History—Partition, 1947. 5. India-Pakistan Conflict, 1947–1949. 6. South Asia—
History—20th century. 7. South Asia—In literature. 8. Authors, Urdu—20th
century—Biography. 9. Short stories, Urdu—History and criticism. 10. Narration
(Rhetoric)—Political aspects—South Asia—History—20th century. I. Title.
    PK2199.H338Z687 2012
    891.4'3936—dc23   2012024142

British Library Cataloging-in-Publication Data is available

This book has been composed in Garamond Premier Pro

Printed on acid-free paper. ∞

Printed in the United States of America

10 9 8 7 6 5 4 3 2 1

In loving memory of Safia Khala—
a wonderful aunt, caring mother,
and gentle-mannered soul
who stoically stood by Manto
through his highs and lows.

Contents

Preface

"This letter comes to you from your Pakistani nephew whom you do not know, nor does anyone else in your land of seven freedoms," Saadat Hasan Manto wrote in the first of a series of factitious letters to Uncle Sam.[1] It was the height of the Cold War. Pakistan was on the verge of signing a military pact with the United States of America. Manto was irked by the prospect of seeing his newly adopted country exchange the ills of British colonialism for the uncertain virtues of American imperialism. In his youth he had imagined driving the British out of India with homemade bombs. He once started a rumor that the British had sold the Taj Mahal to the Americans, who were sending special equipment to Agra to relocate the monument to New York. Within a matter of hours, his hometown, Amritsar, was abuzz with chatter about the sale of the Taj Mahal.[2] With his imaginative canard, Manto gave vent to his anticolonialism while at the same time deftly planting in the minds of subjugated Indians the idea of Britain's declining clout as the dominant global power.

Who was Saadat Hasan Manto, and why is he relevant to a book about the partition of India? The leading Urdu short story writer of the twentieth century, Manto witnessed the psychological trauma of 1947 at close quarters. His sensitive portrayal of the plight of uprooted humanity on the move, in his fictional and nonfictional accounts of partition, is unsurpassed in quality. Charged with obscenity by both the colonial and the postcolonial states for his brutally honest depictions of everyday life, he was condemned in conservative social circles for daring to write about prostitution and sexuality. Manto enthusiasts acclaim him as a genius and a fearless rebel who defied conventions to drive home some plain and awkward truths. Alcoholism killed Saadat Hasan prematurely, but Manto lives on. His work, spanning two decades of prolific writing, is a treasure trove of rare insights into human nature. While much has been written about him and his life from a literary perspective, and several of his short stories are available in English and Hindi, as well as in Japanese, Manto—the writer and the individual in the context of his times—is strikingly underrecognized.[3] His birth centenary year in 2012 lends added urgency to the need to discover and disseminate Manto to the larger international community.

My personal discovery was unavoidable. I have called him Manto Abajan (father) since my childhood, though he had passed away a year before I was born. He was my father's maternal uncle and married to my mother's elder sister, Safia, to whom I was especially close. This book is dedicated to her memory. I still remember Safia Khala (aunt) slipping away quietly by the side door to buy my favorite sweets from Amritsari on Beadon Road, since I would have kept her from going had she left by the front door. My widowed aunt lived with her mother and three daughters in the same mansion block in Lahore as we did. I grew up with Manto's conspicuously absent presence in our joint family and was intrigued by his short stories, several of which I knew before I had learned to read. A personal favorite was his partition classic "Toba Tek Singh," whose main character's prattle fascinated me as a child. The story's dramatic ending made me want to know more about partition. I sensed then that my bond with Manto Abajan transcended the family relationship. It would be several years before I enrolled in a doctoral program in history at the University of Cambridge. I chose to study the causes of India's partition and the creation of Pakistan. Manto's short stories on partition informed my years as a graduate student. My granduncle's literary talents had spotlighted the consequences of partition for ordinary people. As a student of history, I pursued a range of questions that partly move away from this focus, even though I was keenly interested in unearthing the historical evidence on what led to the colossal human tragedy captured so sensitively in Manto Abajan's partition stories.

Manto's keen insights had great resonance for me while I was researching and writing *The Sole Spokesman: Jinnah, the Muslim League and the Demand for Pakistan* (Cambridge, 1985) and *Self and Sovereignty: Individual and Community in South Asian Islam since 1850* (Routledge, 2000). The more I read of Manto, the more impelled I was to write about him one day. It was just a question of timing. When my sister-in-law mentioned something about her father's letters to his mother, my ears pricked up. I was soon helping her organize Manto's papers. These include letters written to him by relatives, friends, and admirers; handwritten manuscripts; and a collection of photographs. I knew there was a book here on

University's History Department backed the project enthusiastically. A special thanks is due to Annette Lazzara, the department administrator, for making life much easier than it would be without her. My warm thanks are due to Dan Rodgers and his colleagues at the Davis Center for asking me to deliver these important annual lectures. Gyan Prakash gave a wonderful introduction to my second lecture, and I benefited from my intellectual exchanges with him. I greatly enjoyed my conversations at Princeton with Jeremy Adelman, David Cannadine, and Linda Colley. Special appreciation is also due to Iftikhar Arif at the National Language Authority in Islamabad, photography aficionado Akhtar Mirza in Lahore, the matchless collector Hameed Haroon at the Dawn Group, and Syed Akbar Hyder at the University of Texas–Austin for giving me access to images and materials for the book. Brigitta van Rheinberg, my editor at Princeton University Press, was supportive of the project from the outset. She gave me good advice during the critical final stages of refining the manuscript.

Friends across the globe have taken an interest in this project and applauded my decision to finally turn to writing on Manto. Nilufer Kuyas in Istanbul has been awaiting the book with an anticipation that is heartwarming. Sunny in London was the first to mention the new word "frenemy" when I told her about Manto's frequent use of "enemy friend." Nita Nazir, also in London, has been a solid friend throughout. In Pakistan, Amber Sami and Naazish Atuallah, among others, have cheered me along while I was researching and writing the book. Amber arranged a reading of the entire manuscript, providing me with a captive audience and allowing me to make useful corrections to the manuscript. This book would have been impossible without my family's support and cooperation. I am indebted to my mother, as ever, for her prayers and confidence in my endeavors. She gave me insights into her brother-in-law that I would never have known otherwise. My brother related several anecdotes about Manto Abajan to me. My sister, who relishes being mistakenly identified as one of Manto's three daughters because of a photograph portraying her with two of them and him, has taken a keen interest in this book. Manto's two elder daughters, Nighat and Nuzhat, have helped me in every way they could. So did Manto's niece, Farida, who went out of her way to find me old photographs, including a priceless one of her mother taken by Manto. My mother's sister-in-law Surriya, whom I call Mamijan (uncle's wife), with her prodigious memory, recounted several incidents relating to Manto Abajan's and Safia Khala's life.

My greatest debt for this book is to Manto's youngest daughter, my sister-in-law Nusrat. If not for her diligent safekeeping of her father's personal papers, I might never have gained access to the Manto archive. She was an invaluable resource in my attempts to negotiate Manto's work and identify some of the more significant writings on him. This book is a product of her unflinching support that has included reading the entire manuscript and pointing out some transliteration errors and other mistakes. Sugata Bose has remained a loyal supporter and constructive critic. We have over the years discussed Manto at length and the reasons for my writing about him one day. He was especially enthusiastic about my framing the Stone Lectures on Manto's life and work, and was instrumental in my calling them "The Pity of Partition." He has patiently seen this work from its inception to the conclusion and made several helpful suggestions.

Researching on Manto Abajan has been quite a revelation; there were so many aspects of his personality, life, and work that I did not know. The experience was immensely rewarding, and I am gratified to be able to bring this book out on the occasion of his birth centenary. Manto had planned to publish a book based on his friends' recollections of him so that readers could get a close and personal view of what he was really like. Inspired by a couplet by the late nineteenth-century Urdu poet Mirza Asadullah Khan Ghalib, Manto referred to the task as a "nail's debt," meaning no debt at all, which his friends owed him. Whether he would consider his grandniece's debt to him as paid will sadly never be known.

The Pity of Partition

dence. "Now before our eyes lie dried tracks of blood, cut up human parts, charred faces, mangled necks, terrified people, looted houses, burned fields, mountains of rubble, and overflowing hospitals. We are free. Hindustan is free. Pakistan is free, and we are walking the desolate streets naked without any possessions in utter distress." Food was scarce and essential commodities were expensive. There was famine. Diseases were spreading. There was no fire in the winter and no water in the summer. The earth was scorched; the skies had receded. Everyone was busy trying to tackle the myriad social problems arising from India's division and the creation of Pakistan. But there was a great deal of noise and very little actual work.[2]

These observations about the depressing aftershocks of partition have a resonance well beyond India. The end of modern colonial empires in the twentieth century, more often then not, has been accompanied by cataclysmic events of partition, civil war, or balkanization. This general tendency can be gleaned from the social and political processes set off by British decolonization in not just India but also Ireland and Palestine. These decisions to divide and quit were taken in the absence of any agreement on power-sharing arrangements among different claimants to the imperial mantle, resulting in unprecedented and tragic violence at the time of independence, as well as a long aftermath of war and conflict. Justified as a necessary evil to avert greater unrest and violence, partition has been an uncertain instrument of conflict management and a veritable barrier to conflict resolution. The destabilizing effects of partition have been writ large on the politics of Ireland, India, Pakistan, Bangladesh, and Palestine, with no respite in sight. Whatever the specific calculations and compulsions of the main political actors, the dislocations and disruptions of partition were ultimately borne by ordinary and mostly innocent men, women, and children. Poets, creative writers, artists, and filmmakers have captured the pity of partition—quite as much as the pity of war—for defenseless people far more effectively than have academic historians bound by their disciplinary conventions.

A historical portrayal of the human tragedy that was India's partition through an innovative exploration of stories, memories, and histories can creatively trespass across the border between fictional and historical narratives. The life and literature of Saadat Hasan Manto form a particularly good point of reference. He is best known internationally for his partition stories, notably "Toba Tek Singh," in which the non-Muslim patients of a mental asylum in Lahore agitatedly await relocation to India because of their religious affiliation.[3] Portraying the inmates to be of sounder mind than those making the decisions for their removal, Manto deftly questioned the wisdom of partition and the sheer madness it had let loose. His partition stories were based on information gleaned from visits to refugee camps and what he learned about the plight of fleeing humanity as he sat in newspaper offices, coffeehouses, and smoke-filled bars. Amidst the darkening shadows of criminality, avarice, and lust, he plumbed the psychological depths of his characters in search of some residual goodness that could help restore faith in human beings. An imaginative inquiry into Manto's personal and literary biography enables an expansion of the historiographical apparatus deployed thus far in explaining the causes and narrating the experiences of partition.

India's partition along ostensibly religious lines in 1947 is simply the most dramatic instance of postwar decolonization based on arbitrary redrawing of boundaries. The forced migration of an estimated fourteen and a half million people, and the murder of perhaps two million innocent men, women, and children, devastated subcontinental psyches. Painful memories of displacement and the horrific killing of kith and kin left deep psychological scars that have not healed. These traumatic memories have fueled hostile relations between India and Pakistan, compounding the difficulties in resolving disputes like Kashmir and the sharing of Himalayan river waters. Partition has only accentuated the problem of identity for Muslims. Although Pakistan was created as a Muslim homeland, fewer Muslims live there than in India or Bangladesh. Memories foregrounding religious differences and the violence perpetrated in their name run the risk of erasing other forms of belonging and sharing cutting across communitarian lines. A defining moment that is neither beginning nor end, partition continues to influence how the peoples and states of postcolonial South Asia envisage their past, present, and future. There can be no real understanding of India, Pakistan, and Bangladesh without a full grasp of the lasting impact of partition on their self-imaginings, political contestations, and national projections.

More than a quarter of a century ago, the publication of my book *The Sole Spokesman: Jinnah, the Muslim League and the Demand for Pakistan* (Cambridge, 1985) pioneered a fresh approach to the high politics that led to the division of the subcontinent into India and Pakistan. Based mainly on official British sources and the documents of the All-India Muslim League (AIML), the study challenged conventional assumptions about the causes of India's partition. The British decision to split up India had usually been attributed to irreconcilable religious differences between Hindus and Muslims, and the intransigence of the Muslim League leader, Mohammad Ali Jinnah. I showed in *The Sole Spokesman* that the end result of partition must not be confused with the aims of Jinnah and the Muslim League to win an equitable share of power for the subcontinent's Muslims.

Far from solving India's Hindu-Muslim problems, partition and the creation of Pakistan exacerbated tensions between the two communities, now split into two hostile nation-states, and complicated the issue of Muslim identity in postcolonial South Asia. When India was partitioned, there were approximately a hundred million Muslims in the subcontinent, more than one person in five. Of these, sixty million became citizens of Pakistan, both east and west, making it the largest Muslim state in the world, but one whose western and eastern wings were separated by over a thousand miles of Indian territory. Some forty million Muslims were left inside India, making them the largest Muslim minority in a non-Muslim state. The disjunction between identity, territory, and sovereignty makes plain that if Indian Muslims had a common faith and a shared religiously informed cultural identity, they were not a geographically distinct or homogenous community with a coherent or united political worldview.

The lack of congruence between the frontiers of modern states and the fuzzy contours of multiple and overlapping identities at the social base is not peculiar to South Asia. Colonial gerrymandering, for strategic and political purposes, has left enduring legacies in large swaths of Asia and Africa with withering effects for their polities and societies. While a longer history of social discord has played a role, the hastily drawn frontiers of Western decolonization have often been the principal cause of volatility in many parts of the postcolonial world. Nowhere has the disconnect between claims to nationhood and the achievement of territorial statehood been more glaring than in a subcontinent ostensibly divided on the basis of religion for the first time in its history. The breakaway of Bangladesh—the former eastern wing of Pakistan—in 1971 was achieved after a bitterly fought fratricidal war in which the massacre of Muslims by Muslims was cut short by India's military intervention. If religion was indeed the primary driving force in the partition of India, it proved to be utterly irrelevant twenty-four years later to the political dynamics that led to the emergence of Bangladesh.

Those averse to privileging religion in explanations of India's partition have tended to blame Jinnah's difficult personality and ill-conceived politics for the peculiar outcome. This has been the wont of official Indian "secular" nationalist historiography and some British apologists of empire. Paradoxically, Jinnah, known as the Quaid-i-Azam (great leader), is also held responsible for partition by his followers, who otherwise revere him as the father of Pakistan. A staunch anticolonial nationalist who made a successful career as a barrister in Bombay, Jinnah started his political life firmly on the side of the Indian National Congress. Upon joining the Muslim League in 1913, he made it clear that his membership in that organization would in no way detract from his loyalty to the Congress and commitment to securing independence from the British. Even after parting company with the Congress following disagreements with Mohandas Karamchand Gandhi and Jawaharlal Nehru, Jinnah lost none of his enthusiasm for the cause of freedom. After the late 1930s, disillusionment with the Congress leadership and the conflicting interests of his Muslim constituents led him to change tactics without abandoning the goal of winning independence for Indians. Afraid that the Congress would swindle Muslims out of any substantial power after the British had departed, Jinnah insisted on a prior constitutional agreement to safeguard Muslim interests in an independent India.

With the outbreak of war in Europe, the British viceroy pressed Jinnah to spell out the Muslim demands to justify rejecting Congress's unrealistic call for immediate independence as the price for its cooperation in the war effort. In March 1940 the AIML at Lahore formally passed a resolution demanding the creation of independent states in the northwest and northeast of India. There was no mention of partition or "Pakistan," an acronym coined by a Muslim student at Cambridge University in the early thirties out of *P*unjab, *Af*ghanistan, *K*ashmir, *S*indh, and Baluchi*stan*, literally meaning land of the pure. Dismissed out of hand by key Muslim politicians, "Pakistan" came to be associated, by sections of the Hindu-owned press, with Muslim separatism and was a provocation for Indian nationalists. They "fathered this word upon us," Jinnah was to tell the AIML three years later.[4] A close examination of the AIML's Lahore resolution reveals considerable ambiguity on the issue of separatism. Vagueness on such a key issue was necessitated by the realities of Muslim politics and demography in India. Muslim politicians in the majority provinces favored a weak center and strong provinces. This offered no comfort for Muslims in provinces where Hindus outnumbered them. Without their coreligionists in the majority provinces backing a Muslim party at a relatively strong center, minority-province Muslims could not hope to redress their provincial imbalances. Content to simply strengthen the provincial autonomy conferred upon them under the 1935 constitution, the Muslim-majority provinces had resoundingly rejected the AIML in the 1937 elections. So while plumping for independent Muslim states based on the grouping of fully autonomous provinces in the northwest and the northeast, the resolution envisaged no center of any kind—a telling omission given that Jinnah's main interest lay with constitutional arrangements at the all-India center.

Grounding itself on the principle of self-determination as enunciated by the American president Woodrow Wilson, the essence of the AIML's demand was that by international standards Indian Muslims were not a minority but a nation entitled to exercise sovereignty over areas where they were in the majority. The separatist thrust of the claim was dented by reference in the resolution's fourth paragraph to a "constitution," in the singular, to safeguard the rights of all minorities. This implied openness to negotiating a constitutional arrangement covering the whole of India. Leaving the question of the all-India constitutional structure for later negotiations, Jinnah in the remaining years of World War II insisted that the principle of "Pakistan," the territorial embodiment of the Muslim claim to nationhood, had to be conceded prior to any decisions concerning the shape and powers of any future all-India center. Arguing that the Indian unitary center would stand dissolved at the moment of the British withdrawal, he maintained that any renegotiated center—unitary, federal, or confederal—had to be based on the agreement of all the constituent units, including the Muslim-majority provinces and the princely states that accounted for nearly 40 percent of the subcontinental land mass.

Once the British and the Congress agreed to the principle of "Pakistan," Jinnah was prepared to discuss whether the proposed Muslim state would forge a confederal relationship with the rest of India or enter into treaty arrangements on matters of common interest between two essentially sovereign states—Pakistan (representing the Muslim-majority provinces) and Hindustan (representing the Hindu-majority provinces). In either case, Jinnah wanted something close to parity with the Congress at the all-India level since Muslims as a nation had a right to an equal share of power with the Hindus. If it was to cover the interests of Muslims in both the majority and the minority provinces, "Pakistan" had to remain part of an all-India whole. Jinnah and the AIML expected "Pakistan" to be carved out of the existing Muslim provinces, which meant that there would be large non-Muslim minorities in the independent Muslim states. Unless the existing shape of the two main-Muslim majority provinces of Punjab and Bengal was preserved, Jinnah and the Muslim League could not hope to negotiate reciprocal safeguards for both sets of minorities visualized in the Lahore resolution.

Self-determination for the Muslims of India could not be denied to non-Muslims in the territories claimed for Pakistan. The specifically Muslim nature of the Pakistan demand had alienated non-Muslims. As the endgame drew near, the British and the Congress refused to countenance Pakistan in any shape or form without giving non-Muslims in the eastern and western districts of Punjab and Bengal, where they were in the majority, the right to choose their future. This was anathema to Jinnah, whose strategy depended on using the weight of undivided Punjab and Bengal to negotiate a substantial share of power at the all-India level in order to cover the interests of all Muslims. Once the British had made up their minds to leave, Jinnah and the AIML were given the choice of a sovereign Pakistan consisting of western Punjab and eastern Bengal or a three-tiered federal structure for undivided India with no firm guarantee of the Muslim share at the center. Under the proposed federal scheme, provinces were to be grouped together into three sections at the second tier, with the center confined to defense, foreign affairs, and communications. Firmly opposed to the partition of Punjab and Bengal, Jinnah could see that grouping would allow the AIML to use the combined force of the Muslim provinces to offset the Congress's majority at the federal level. If the arrangement failed to work within a stipulated period of ten years, groups of provinces could decide to opt out.

A brilliant constitutional lawyer, Jinnah could detect more merits in the federal framework for united India than in the sovereign Pakistan on offer. In 1944 the veteran Congress leader from Madras, C. R. Rajagopalachari, had suggested a "Pakistan" based on a partition of Punjab and Bengal along religious lines. Slamming the idea as a parody of the original Muslim demand, Jinnah famously dubbed it a "maimed, mutilated and moth-eaten" state.[5] Two years later in June 1946, at their leader's behest the AIML rejected a sovereign Pakistan created out of western Punjab and eastern Bengal, and instead agreed to the proposed federal arrangements. Nehru's public refusal to accept the grouping of provinces and restrictions on the powers of the center forced the AIML to revert to the demand for a sovereign Pakistan. Once the British categorically refused to concede undivided Punjab and Bengal to the Muslim League, Jinnah had no choice but to acquiesce in the creation of a Pakistan whose geographical boundaries he had spurned twice over the preceding three years.

My analysis of Jinnah's real aims in orchestrating the Muslim demand for Pakistan was initially characterized as "revisionist." However, in contending that the AIML's claim of Indian Muslim nationhood was not an inevitable overture to separate sovereign statehood, it articulated a position that was soon embraced as the new orthodoxy on the causes of India's partition. Since then, there has been a plethora of scholarly and popular works on partition. Some of these have focused on related aspects of the final decades of the struggle between the forces of Indian nationalism and British colonialism. In *Self and Sovereignty: Individual and Community in South Asian Islam since 1850* (Routledge, 2000), I revisited the politics of partition through a close study of the interplay of nation, religion, and region in the construction of communitarian discourses about Muslim identity, with special reference to Punjab. My analysis of partition violence demonstrated how "banded individuals" rather than entire communities were the perpetrators, even if vulnerable communities were the victims. Drawing a distinction between religion as faith and religion as a demarcator of identity, I questioned the all-too-easy attribution of "communal violence" to religious zeal. Three potent factors—*zan* (women), *zar* (wealth), and *zamin* (land)—ingrained in the material and patriarchal culture of rural Punjab played a critical role in shaping the nature of the violence that engulfed the region in 1947.[6] There have been several other studies over the past decade and a half reflecting a shift away from the all-India level to the regions, scholarship that has helped refine understandings of both Indian anticolonial nationalism and the politics of communitarian identity during the final decades of the British raj in India. At the same time a number of works have tried to foreground the personal narratives of pain and trauma by privileging fiction and memory in an evident attempt to critique colonial masters. By illuminating the complexities of Hindu-Muslim relations in cities such as Bombay, the stories and letters read together supply new insights into urban history and everyday cosmopolitanism in late colonial India. It is against this backdrop that Manto's fictional narratives of partition so vividly and impartially capture the historical nuances of the human tragedy occasioned by the catastrophic breakdown in communitarian relations at the end of the British raj.

The genre of memory studies that has been much in vogue in the last two decades has serious pitfalls. There are both general problems associated with excavating individual and collective memories of traumatic events, such as the Holocaust, and specific shortcomings of South Asian works on memories drawing upon the violence and dislocations of partition. Privileging memories shaped by violent ruptures cannot but provide a distorting prism for looking into the history of the entire gamut of social and political relations. Such an approach not only subsumes individual experiences into collective memories but also ends up folding communitarian remembrances into the straitjacket of official nationalist narratives. Resorting to the trauma of the Holocaust as a universal model creates problems of another kind. Even though the late colonial and postcolonial states cannot escape culpability for the massive mayhem that accompanied decolonization in the subcontinent, the murderous communitarian rivalries of that era were a distance removed from the state-orchestrated "final solution." Memory studies of partition in the South Asian context have not only influenced understandings of later episodes of violence, such as the anti-Sikh pogroms of 1984 and Hindu-Muslim conflicts of 1992 and 2002, but have also borne their deep imprint. The second chapter of this book marks a radical

the Baghdad Pact—the book evokes the continuing contemporary relevance and lasting legacy of the historical conjuncture represented by the moment of partition and its immediate aftermath. An acute observer of the present, Saadat Hasan Manto had an uncanny ability to foresee the future. His ruminations as well as razor-sharp insights into religion and hypocrisy, the multiple meanings of martyrdom, the vexed uncle-nephew relationship between America and Pakistan, and, above all, the confused and overlapping identities of the rival siblings that replaced the British raj afford the historian a wealth of materials to weave together the past, present, and future of a subcontinent's predicaments.

I

Stories

"Nothing but the Truth"

"Knives, Daggers, and Bullets Cannot Destroy Religion"

Bombay was rife with fear and foreboding. The British had wielded the partitioner's ax. Reports of horrific bloodletting in northern India, particularly Punjab, had turned the cosmopolitan city into a battleground of real and imagined hostilities along purportedly religious lines. Four good Punjabi friends, three Hindus and one Muslim, were parting company. Mumtaz was going to Pakistan, a country he neither knew nor felt anything for. His decision to leave was sudden but unsurprising. Relatives of his Hindu friends in western Punjab had suffered loss of life and property. Overcome with grief upon hearing of his uncle's murder by Muslim gangs in Lahore, Jugal had told Mumtaz that he would kill him if violence broke out in their neighborhood. After eight days of stoic silence, Mumtaz announced that he was setting sail for Karachi within a few hours.

Jugal fell into a deep silence. Mumtaz became excessively talkative; he started drinking incessantly and packing as if departing for a picnic. When the time came for him to leave, they all took a taxi to the port, which was bustling with mostly destitute refugees heading for Pakistan. As they stood on the deck of the ship sipping brandy, Jugal begged Mumtaz to forgive him. When Mumtaz asked whether he really meant that he could kill him, Jugal replied in the affirmative and apologized. "You would have been sorrier if you had killed me," Mumtaz asserted philosophically, "though only if you had realized that it wasn't Mumtaz, a Muslim and a friend of yours, whom you had killed but a human being. If he had been a bastard, you would have killed him, not the bastard in him; and if he had been a Muslim, you would have killed him, not his Muslimness. If his corpse had fallen into Muslim hands, the graveyard would have an additional grave but the world would have one human being less." "It is possible that my co-religionists would call me a martyr," Mumtaz continued, "but I swear upon God, I will leap out of my grave and refuse a degree for which I took no exam." "Muslims in Lahore killed your uncle and you killed me in Bombay. What medal do you or I deserve? What medal is your uncle's killer in Lahore worthy of? I would say that those who died, died a dog's death and those who killed, killed in vain."

Becoming more emotional, Mumtaz explained that by religion he really meant the faith that distinguishes human beings from beasts of prey. "Don't say that a hundred thousand Hindus and a hundred thousand Muslims have been massacred," he told his friends. "Say that two hundred thousand human beings have perished. The great tragedy is not that two hundred thousand people have been killed. What is tragic is that the loss of life has been futile. Muslims who killed a hundred thousand Hindus might think they had eradicated Hinduism, but it is alive and will remain alive.

Similarly, the Hindus who murdered one hundred thousand Muslims may rejoice at the death of Islam when actually Islam has not been affected in the least bit. Those who think religion can be hunted down with guns are stupid. Religion, faith, belief, devotion are matters of the spirit, not of the body. Knives, daggers, and bullets cannot destroy religion."[1] Mumtaz then related the story of Sahai, a staunch Hindu fastidious in his habits and a paragon of ethical behavior despite making a living as a pimp. Sahai had come to Bombay from Madras to make enough money to launch his own retail cloth business. Caring and honest to a fault, he had opened accounts for each of the girls who worked for him. One day soon after the troubles began, Mumtaz found Sahai bleeding to death on the footpath in the Muslim locality of Bhindi Bazaar. Afraid of being implicated in the murder, Mumtaz considered running away. But the dying man called out his name and gave him a packet containing ornaments and money for a Muslim prostitute, Sultana. Mumtaz duly delivered the packet to a teary-eyed Sultana, along with her patron's message urging her to leave for a safer place. After his Hindu friends disembarked from the ship, Mumtaz waved at them from the deck. One of them thought Mumtaz was waving at Sahai, eliciting Jugal's wistful reply: "I wish I were Sahai."[2]

There was evidently no dearth of Sahais in a Bombay otherwise imploding with pent-up frustrations and newfound hatred against other religious communities. A scrupulously honest and hardworking Hindu washerman, Ram Khalawan, refused to keep account of what he washed for a newlywed Muslim couple. He was indebted to the man's elder brother, for whom he had worked for several years. The couple repaid his faith in both cash and kind. When he fell grievously ill after drinking poisonous alcohol, the wife took Khalawan to a doctor by taxi. He survived the ordeal and quit drinking altogether, which was not easy for someone who had to stand in water for hours on end everyday. After his wife had left for Lahore following partition and the outbreak of violence, the husband noticed that Khalawan had hit the bottle again. Once the situation in the city became untenable, he too decided to leave for Lahore. Since his clothes were with the washerman, he decided to fetch them before the curfew. As he approached the washermen's colony, he saw a group of inhabitants dancing with long heavy wooden sticks in their hands. They were all reeling drunk. He inquired whether they knew Ram Khalawan and was asked whether he was a Hindu or a Muslim. "I am a Muslim," he said. "Kill him, kill him," was the response. He caught sight of an inebriated Ram Khalawan, barely able to stay on his feet but wielding a fat stick and cursing Muslims. He called out the name of the laundryman, who initially raised his stick to hit him. Then all of a sudden, Khalawan stopped in his tracks and blurted out, "Sahib!" Gathering himself together, he told his carousing companions: "He is not a Muslim; he is my Sahib, Begum Sahib's Sahib. . . . she came in a motor car. . . . took me to see a doctor. . . . who treated me." The words failed to have any effect, and the washermen almost came to blows as they began arguing among themselves. Seeing his chance, the narrator of the story quietly slipped away. The next day, as he awaited the delivery of his ticket, the doorbell rang. It was Ram Khalawan, carrying a bundle of his freshly washed clothes. "You are leaving, Sahib?" he asked, teary faced. Begging forgiveness, he disclosed that weathy men in the city were inciting people to kill Muslims by plying them with free alcohol. Who could resist free alcohol? For the nth time Khalawan recounted all the favors the narrator, his wife, and his generous elder brother had bestowed upon him. He then shouldered the empty cloth in which he had carried the washed clothing and walked out the door.[3]

Neither of the two stories is typical of narratives foregrounding the ghastly carnage and human suffering that accompanied the partition of India. Authored by the acknowledged master of the Urdu short story, Saadat Hasan Manto, they do not glorify or demonize any community. There is no attempt to articulate a moral resolution to the unfolding tragedy or to escape it through nostalgic remembrances of a harmonious social milieu in the distant past. Partly autobiographical, both stories efface the distinction between fictional and historical narratives and, together with the broader corpus of his better-known partition stories, establish a riveting symbiosis between Manto's life and work at the moment of an agonizing historical rupture. For someone who liked to keep his ear close to the ground in order to weave tales out of facts gleaned from everyday life, Manto, the individual and writer, is ideal fare for the historian of partition. An astute witness to his times, Manto crafted stories that give a more immediate and penetrating account of those troubled and troubling times than do most journalistic accounts of partition.

Creative writers have captured the human dimensions of partition far more effectively than have historians. Manto excelled in this genre with the searching power of his observation, the pace of his storytelling, and the facility and directness of his language. Unlike others who have written stories about partition violence to condemn its oppressive and dehumanizing characteristics, he was patently uninterested in its outward manifestations. Manto used his literary talent to reflect the consequences of partition for the lives of common people. He knew that cataclysmic events make the unusual seem ordinary. Nothing shocks the human consciousness numbed by displays of human bestiality amidst massive social dislocation. Ethical issues become irrelevant, and writing about them, whether as fiction or historical narrative, fails to make the news. Without making any kind of a value judgment, Manto wrote short stories that were not about violence as such but about people and their different faces. The perpetrators and the victims of their oppression interest him only insofar as they help to lay bare the all-too-human characteristics that can momentarily turn the gentlest of souls into the most demonic monsters. Neither an end nor a beginning, partition—with its multifaceted ruptures, political and psychological—was for Manto not an aberration to be dismissed as a fleeting collective madness. It was part and parcel of an unfolding drama that gave glimpses into the best and the worst in humankind. Through his close-range and personal picture of characters like Jugal, Sahai, Ram Khalawan, and unnamed murderers, Manto turns short story writing into a testament of his belief that human depravity, though real and pervasive, can never succeed in killing all sense of humanity. His faith lay in that kind of humanity.

What made Manto possible? His literary corpus is the best place to begin searching for an approximate answer. Proud and prone to displays of arrogance, he had a high opinion of his talent and place in history. Manto has been

1
Manto writing, by Khatir Ghaznavi,
Lahore, 1954. Courtesy Pakistan
Academy of Letters, Government of
Pakistan, Islamabad

likened to Guy de Maupassant, not for consciously seeking to emulate the French short story writer but because, like him, he aimed at exposing societal ills and the hypocrisies of life without losing faith in the inherent beauty within human beings.[4] Manto was deeply affected by Jean-Jacques Rousseau's observation that man is born free but is everywhere in chains. To convey his thoughts and feelings on the matter, he taught himself the fundamentals of storytelling by reading and translating French and Russian writers like Maupassant, Zola, Hugo, Chekhov, Tolstoy, and many others. Later his exposure to Somerset Maugham, O. Henry, and D. H. Lawrence encouraged him to write about issues of sexuality in ways that were new and often disturbing for a segment of the Urdu readership. Despite this exposure to international literature, Manto in his choice of themes and linguistic techniques remained steeped in the literary traditions of the subcontinent. His unique traits notwithstanding, Manto is a good example of those writers from the colonized world whose universalist aspirations and cosmopolitan attitudes were rooted in regional languages, literatures, and cultures.

Manto's subjects were actual people faced with real-life issues whom he searched for in the dark and stinking alleyways of the cities he lived in and visited with friends in search of alcohol and entertainment.[5] His most memorable characters are products of the illicit social exchanges that take place in these filthy and ill-famed urban neighborhoods. Whether he was writing about prostitutes, pimps, or criminals, Manto wanted to impress on his readers that these disreputable people were also human, much more so than those who cloaked their failings in a thick veil of hypocrisy. Irony and paradox were two formidable elements in his repertoire of literary devices that enabled him and his readers to see through that veil. Manto's brand of literary humanism was shaped by multiple literary and cultural milieus—both global and regional. If an engagement with global literature of the French and Russian varieties honed his literary craft, his habitation of modernity was inflected by his location in a world of colonial difference, as well as myriad internal differences fostered by an alien colonial rule. Few writers were as adept as Saadat Hasan Manto at uncovering the everyday cosmopolitanism that transcended those differences. Exuding a sense of destiny that often surprised his peers, he made sure to leave behind an extraordinarily rich archive of insights into his life, personality, and writings. As he wryly commented in one of his typical tongue-in-cheek autobiographical pieces, it was quite "possible that Saadat Hasan dies and Manto lives on," but that would be like an eggshell minus the white and the yolk.[6] He dreaded nothing more than the prospect of Saadat Hasan's living on while Manto died.

The name Manto comes from the Kashmiri word *mant*, meaning a stone weighing one and a half seer, or approximately three pounds, and is thought to refer to what his Saraswat Brahman ancestors were entitled to collect as rent from the cultivating peasants.[7] Proud of his Kashmiri background, Manto claimed that *mant* referred to the scale in which his ancestors' wealth was weighed. In a play on his own name, he once quipped that he was a "one two man," who added up to three. If he hid his head and neck like a tortoise, however, no one could detect, far less understand, him. Critics wrote long essays on how he was influenced by Schopenhauer, Freud, Hegel, Nietzsche, and Marx, when

Amritsar Dreams of Revolution

Saadat Hasan Manto was born a hundred years ago on May 11, 1912, at Sambrala in Ludhiana District. His Kashmiri Muslim trading family had migrated to Punjab in the early nineteenth century and eventually settled down in Amritsar. After abandoning their traditional trade in Kashmiri pashmina shawls for the legal profession, Manto's ancestors took up residence in Amritsar's Koocha Vakilaan, the Lawyers' Colony. Manto's mother, Sardar Begum, was the second wife of his father, Khwaja Ghulam Hasan. A trained lawyer who rose to become a sessions judge in the government of Punjab's Justice Department, Ghulam Hasan was a strictly practicing Muslim who, in his spare time, penned works on Islam and the real meaning of jihad. He had three sons and six daughters from his first wife. Sardar Begum had a Pathan ancestry. After being orphaned at the age of nine, she was married into a well-off family in Amritsar, who brought her up with exemplary care and consideration. Her first marriage was never consummated. The husband resented being saddled with an underage wife and showed no interest in her even after she turned twenty-one. He started

2
Manto's father,
Khwaja Ghulam Hasan
(1855–1932)

leading a life of decadence, forcing his own family to consider marrying their young ward to a relative with a better sense of responsibility. Sardar Begum's first husband was strongly averse to her marrying within his family. So he arranged for her marriage to an acquaintance, Ghulam Hasan, whose first wife was prone to fits of mental instability.[8]

Sardar Begum gave birth to four children, of whom only Saadat and his sister Nasira Iqbal survived. Ghulam Hasan wanted his youngest son to become a doctor, equaling if not surpassing the achievements of his elder sons, who were studying in England. Muhammad and Saeed qualified as barristers, while Salim became an engineer. Having spent a fortune educating his three elder sons abroad, Manto's father had little left for the upkeep of his second wife and her children, who lived separately from the rest of the family in a small section of the house. Saadat's elementary education in Arabic, Persian, Urdu, and English was completed at home under his father's watchful eye. Ghulam Hasan's eagerness to see Saadat excel in his studies flowed from a desire that the extended family should change its low opinion of his second wife, who, contrary to tradition, came from outside the Manto clan.

The contempt shown by the paternal side of the family for his mother left a deep emotional scar. A sensitive and highly

3
Manto's mother,
Sardar Begum
(d. 1940)

intelligent child, Saadat resented the differential treatment meted out to his mother. Memories of neglect and rejection shaped his personality, making him prone to excessive displays of emotion. Unable to forge a meaningful relationship with his father, he longed for the approval and affection of his elder brothers, whom he met only after he had become an established Urdu short story writer. His relationship with the brothers was cordial and correct, but never close. Differences in upbringing and age, not to mention their clashing lifestyles, kept them miles apart, emotionally, intellectually, and spiritually. The distance between the siblings was partly bridged by the personal bonds Manto later forged with their children. His need to earn the respect of his elder brothers notwithstanding, Manto was fiercely individualistic and self-confident. If these traits can be credited to the indulgence of a doting mother and sister, the steely discipline of an authoritarian father served as a catalyst for Saadat's rebellious nature.

The rebel in Manto was still terrified of his father. Once while flying a kite on the rooftop instead of studying, he became panic-stricken upon hearing his father's footsteps. To escape the wrath of the family patriarch, Saadat jumped into the courtyard below, hurting himself in the process, but without wincing. He sought no support and cut no corners; he hated those who pleaded for mercy. Kite flying remained an abiding passion for Manto. He frequently jumped off the roof to save his skin, often landing on people's heads and eliciting their fury. Remorseless and belligerent, Manto claimed the right to fly kites since no one had proprietorship of the skies. He threatened to pounce on whoever tried to trip him. If someone cut the string of his kite, he vowed to smash his head with a brick. In this menacing standoff, akin to a game of snakes and ladders, society inflicted several wounds on Manto, who neither complained of victimhood nor appealed for mercy. What he sought was appreciation. His lips were unfamiliar with the art of supplication.[9]

Saadat started his formal schooling in class four at Amritsar's Muslim Anglo-Oriental [M.A.O.] High School. His shenanigans with Khwaja Hasan Abbas, a childhood friend, earned him the nickname "Tommy," a derogatory word denoting a British soldier.[10] Intelligent, gifted, but overflowing with mischief, Manto failed the school-leaving exams three times owing to his lack of affinity for the science subjects his father had forced him to take. Roaming the streets of Amritsar with his friends and dabbling in photography were infinitely more interesting. Saadat even took to developing his own photographs, especially those of his sister and mother, who could not appear unveiled before a male stranger. His burgeoning extracurricular interests meant spending increasingly more time away from school, but they taught him the lessons he wanted to learn from the book of life. He acquired a reputation within the Manto clan for being a slacker, gambler, drinker of alcohol, and inveterate prankster with an interest in occult, an entirely unworthy son of an honorable and respected man. Saadat soon lost interest in gambling, but there was no letup in either his drinking or his mischief making. A contrarian by nature, Manto only strengthened his resolve not to conform or compromise in the face of familial disapproval of his lifestyle. When his father's pressure on him to pass his school-leaving exams became unbearable, Manto decided to drop the science subjects in favor of Persian and Urdu. He switched schools, enrolling in the Muslim High

School. There, in May 1931, he scraped through on the fourth attempt but, remarkably enough, failed in the language that was to become the medium for his rise to fame. His father died a disappointed man nine months later, on 25 February 1932.

Manto's undistinguished educational path turned out to be a blip in the rising graph of a short and spectacular literary career. Outside the constraints of formal schooling he proved to be a swift learner and an avid reader of revolutionary literature. Bristling with anti-British sentiments but skeptical of the Congress and Muslim League leadership, he was captivated by the popular folk hero Bhagat Singh, a radical young Sikh hanged by the British in Lahore in 1931 for killing a police officer and hurling a bomb in the central assembly. This was in keeping with the political mood in Punjab, where there was outrage cutting across the religious divide at Mohandas Karamchand Gandhi's refusal to appeal to the British to commute Bhagat Singh's death sentence. After passing his matriculation exams, Manto joined the Hindu Sabha College, where he was reunited with his M.A.O. High School chum, Hasan Abbas.

The college atmosphere was suffused with excitement over Amritsar's pivotal role in the rising tide of anticolonialism in India ever since 1919. Following Turkey's defeat in World War I, Gandhi joined hands with pro-Khilafat Muslims worried about the future of the Ottoman caliphate. The alliance enabled Gandhi to overcome opposition within the Congress party against launching the noncooperation movement against the Rowlatt Act of 1919—an act that allowed the colonial state to perpetuate wartime emergency ordinances in peacetime. It was at Amristar's Jallianwalla Bagh, a public garden, that the nationalist struggle acquired its best-

4
Manto in Amritsar

remembered martyrs of the noncooperation era. In its aftermath, Bhagat Singh and his associates continued the tradition
of fearless defiance of colonial authority. Inspired by Bhagat

Singh's sacrifice for the nationalist cause, Saadat and Hasan Abbas began fantasizing about becoming revolutionaries and driving the British out of India. Instead of doing their school-work in class ten, they spread out a map of the world and plotted their overland escape route to Moscow long before any of the subcontinent's well-known communist intellectuals had come to light. Amritsar was Moscow for them and its streets the venue where they wanted to see autocratic and oppressive rulers brought down and made to eat humble pie.

Abu Saeed Qureshi joined the two aspiring revolutionaries after initially bonding with them because of their shared passion for Hollywood actresses. Manto was an avid collector of film magazines and posters. Poring over the photographs of their personal favorites transported them from Amritsar to Hollywood in an instant. Saeed recalled first meeting Manto at the shop of a local photographer, Ashiq Ali, who had a dazzling range of cameras and equipment, as well as experience taking portraits of film stars in Bombay. Impressed by the paraphernalia at Ashiq's shop, the trio started getting photographs of their favorite stars framed. When the hobby proved too costly, they bought the appropriate materials and did the framing themselves. Saeed recalls longing for Greta Garbo's forlorn beauty and Saadat's being enchanted by Marlene Dietrich's legs.[11]

Manto's ancestral home in the northern part of the Lawyers' Colony was a modest structure compared to the houses of his better-off relatives. His room near the eastern entrance of the house had north-facing windows. He had evocatively named it Dar-ul-Ahmar, literally the red room. Near the door was a makeshift seat covered by a Multani quilt. His writing table, stacked with books and dominated by a large inkpot in the shape of a motorcar, faced the windows. To the immediate left of the desk was a small almirah (cupboard) full of books, and on the right, a fireplace adorned by Bhagat Singh's bust. The bust was flanked by an oil lamp and an old telephone receiver; after a call he tried to place failed to go through, Manto had pulled the receiver out of a public phone booth, grumbling, "What's this fraud?"[12] The walls of Dar-ul-Ahmar reflected the primary tension in Manto's life. Opposite a wall decorated with posters of Joan Crawford, Marlene Dietrich, and Bhagat Singh was a photograph of his father with large angry eyes, a finely cut moustache, and a beard. Wearing a closed-collar coat and a Kashmiri-style turban, Ghulam Hasan looked on disapprovingly at what was going on in the room.[13]

Life might have continued its gentle drift to nowhere if Manto had not made an extraordinary acquaintance. The decisive moment in his literary career came in April 1933 when, at the age of twenty-one, he met Abdul Bari Alig, a peripatetic socialist journalist-cum-historian. Bari had no degree from Aligarh University but was so proud to be associated with the institution as a result of having studied there that he appended "Alig" to his name. The author of a popular anticolonial history of the English India Company's rule, Bari mostly wrote polemical pieces on Hegel and Marx, or pontificated on the philosophy and poetry of Muhammad Iqbal. Saadat Hasan first encountered his future mentor at the Shiraz Hotel in the company of the acclaimed Urdu poet Akhtar Shirani. Bari was then working for the Amritsar daily *Musawat* (Equality). A student of economics and history, Bari knew nothing of literature, so the discussion drifted to politics. When the question of capital punishment came up, Manto asked Bari for his opinion on the matter. Bari quoted from a speech by Victor Hugo, a part of which had been published in Urdu translation in the Calcutta-based newspaper *Al-Hilal* (Crescent), run by Maulana Abul Kalam Azad. Bari also referred to Hugo's *The Last Day of a Condemned Man*. "I have the book," Saadat chimed in, "would you like to read it again?" The next day he arrived at *Musawat*'s office with the book. As he waited for Bari to complete copyediting, Saadat's eyes wandered off to the line of scribes, a lightbulb hanging over each of them as they wrote the Urdu script on yellow pieces of paper. He was fascinated.[14]

A few days later when Manto returned to *Musawat*'s office, he spotted a press pass for a local cinema lying on Bari's desk. He asked Bari when he was going to see the film. Bari had no interest in the film and offered the pass to Manto on the condition that he write a few lines about it for *Musawat*'s film page. Manto complied and was delighted to see his writing in print the next day. Bari claimed that the publication of those few lines stirred the hidden story writer in Manto. Soon after, Hasan Abbas and Abu Saeed Qureshi met Bari, and they all started meeting for evening walks in Ram Bagh, a park located on the northern edge of Amritsar's famous residential neighborhood, the Civil Lines. After a few more people had joined the group, they decided one night in Ram Bagh to set up a Free Thinkers' circle with some bizarre rules. By way of example, members were expected to wear flannel trousers and khaki shirts in the summer, and to make a fool of someone once a month. All the Free Thinkers except Manto managed to dupe somebody over the course of a month. When the local photographer Ashiq Ali walked into the Shiraz Hotel, Manto sensed his opportunity. Winking at the group, he proceeded to tell Ashiq about the wonders of Lahore, where even the traffic police had been provided with coats made of ice. "Rubbish," Ashiq blurted out. Manto confidently persisted with his lies, noting that if modern science could produce electric fans, there was no reason why ice coats could not be made. Ashiq fell silent and the discussion moved on. The next day at the Shiraz Hotel, as Manto was trying to persuade the Free Thinkers that he had fulfilled the membership requirement of making a fool of somebody, an agitated Ashiq walked in. He had just returned from Lahore. On seeing Manto, he picked up the nearest object he could find and hit him on the head. Manto retaliated with a cup of tea, and they scuffled for some time. When blood started dripping from their faces, they had to be forcibly separated. They made peace and went to the doctor together.[15]

Manto's pranks did not end with this episode. But the Free Thinkers lost momentum and fell to pieces. Bari was drawn to the leftist thought that was beginning to make an impact on Indian politics at the time. Some political workers in Amritsar decided to establish an Anti-Imperialist League on "scientific" principles. Bari was invited to address one of their meetings, held in a dark room in the western part of Jallianwalla Bagh. It was there, on 13 April 1919, that General Reginald Dyer had ordered his men to fire on an unarmed crowd of protesters, killing 379 innocent men, women, and children and injuring over a thousand. Bari understood a mere 20 percent of what was said at the gathering about contemporary politics. However, the experience taught him the importance of the international situation for local politics. Instead of the tomfooleries of the Free Thinkers' circle, he now began promoting serious thinking among his disciples. By then Saadat had translated Hugo's *The Last Day of a Condemned Man* from English into Urdu, and his translation was published a few months later by Urdu Book Stall, Lahore. On Bari's encouragement, Saadat translated Russian and French short stories from English into Urdu for the next three to four years. This helped establish his name as one of the foremost translators in a country where there was a growing market for such works. The success of the endeavor is underlined by the publication of one of his initial translations in the influential literary journal *Humayun*. Bari remembered the surprise and envy that greeted Saadat's emergence as a writer. But Hasan Abbas and Abu Saeed were elated by their friend's achievment and developed an interest in writing.[16]

Manto's room was filled with the works of Victor Hugo, Lord Lytton, Maxim Gorky, Anton Chekhov, Pushkin, Gogol, Dostoyevsky, Leonid Andreyev, Oscar Wilde, and Maupassant. Bari regarded Hugo as the greatest novelist in the world. "We got his writings from far and wide," Abu Saeed recollected, "and read them repeatedly like course books." Bari supervised the trio's translation of one of Oscar Wilde's lesser plays, *Vera*, a melodramatic tragedy about Russian nihilist revolutionaries. The play was printed at a publicity-savvy local press. Life-size posters advertising the book were pasted on the main city walls. The text for the poster, which Bari had excerpted from the play, was open to charges of sedition:

> Autocratic and oppressive rulers meet their dreadful end
> Russia's streets are resonating with cries of vengeance
> Hammering the last nail in the Romanoff dynasty's coffin

Amritsar was seething with political tensions. Arrests were the flavor of the season, and the colonial state's jails were well populated. Passersby only read the headlines; many moved away quickly out of fear of being accused of entertaining ideas of sedition.[17] The posters were promptly removed the following day. Bari quietly slipped away from the scene, and so the police hurled Saadat and Abbas into jail. When the police investigative party came to the Lawyers' Colony and questioned one of Manto's brothers-in-law, a former deputy superintendent of the police, he scolded them: "These are our children, go and do your work." If the police had not heeded the advice of a former colleague and had pursued the child's play with their usual vigor, Abu Saeed mused, "Manto had all the qualities of being a Bhagat Singh."[18]

Timid and cowardly by temperament, Bari was an unlikely mentor for the budding revolutionaries. Apart from his erudition, Bari's main qualification in the eyes of the young men was his personal acquaintance with their hero Bhagat Singh, who, like Bari, came from Lyallpur. Manto recounts how their chosen mentor had a knack for disappearing from the scene if a situation born of his revolutionary ideas and the youthful enthusiasm of his disciples threatened to set the colonial government's coercive machinery into action. He did this with panache before the colonial authorities discovered the *Vera* posters. Several other such incidents showed Bari to be a man of ingenuity, but one lacking the courage of his convictions. "If our guide had not been so spineless," Abu Saeed reflected, "the statuettes of four children playing in the shadows of Bhagat Singh's bust on the fireplace of Dar-ul-Ahmar would have been standing in a gallery alongside Danton, Robespierre, Mazzini, Lenin, and Trotsky."[19] Instead of being incensed by this characteristic and feeling let down by Bari, Manto thought it a godsend, since otherwise they might have all passed into history as the martyrs of Amritsar. He was less forgiving of Bari's other shortcomings. The end of the road for them came after partition, when Manto was put off to find Bari, the quintessential anti-imperialist, meekly working as a lowly employee in the Lahore office of the British High Commission.[20]

As long as they were together in Amritsar, the three friends remained riveted by Bari's extensive knowledge and peculiar imagination. Their liaison gave a much-needed direction to Saadat's disorderly life. He began writing regular film reviews for *Musawat*, in addition to translating Russian and French short stories, an invaluable process that taught him the fundamentals of this genre of writing. Soon afterwards he penned his first short story, "Tamasha," which was published in a weekly literary journal called *Khalq*, established by Bari in Lahore in August 1934. Based on the Jallianwalla Bagh massacre in Amritsar, the story is a moving autobiographical account of what Manto experienced as a seven-year-old on that fateful day of the anticolonial struggle in the subcontinent. Substantiating his oft-repeated claim that he mainly wrote about what he had either witnessed or heard reliable accounts of, Manto recalls the panic he felt at the sight of low-flying planes hovering like black eagles over his home for the third day running. There was anticipation of something bloody in the offing. The bazaars were haunted, and an eerie silence blanketed the entire city. On hearing that the planes were loaded with bombs and might drop a few on them, Khalid (the name Manto gave to his stand-in in the story) clasped his toy gun and began practicing his shots to avenge an attack. He was relieved when instead of bombs the planes dropped pieces of paper announcing a royal prohibition on public meetings and warning of severe consequences if the ban was not heeded. After reading the leaflet, his father turned pale. Upon being prodded, he told Khalid that there was going to be a *tamasha*, or a great spectacle, in the city to which he promised to take his son.

As there was no school that day, nor anyone he could play with, Khalid passed the ensuing hours staring out the window into empty streets. In the afternoon he was sitting with his father and mother in the courtyard when the air moaned with the sound of repeated gunshots. Khalid grabbed his father's hand and said, "Let's go, the spectacle, the game has started." His father shrugged him off, saying there was still plenty of time for the *tamasha*. So Khalid returned to the window to get an update on what was happening in the street below. He heard the sound of dogs wailing in the distance and the agonized cries of human beings. Suddenly he spotted a young boy faltering desperately as he ran down the square screaming, a fountain of blood gushing from the calf of his leg. Khalid saw the boy fall and lose consciousness. He ran to tell his father, who, in deference to the royal prohibition, did not leave the house to help the dying boy. There were any number of armored government vehicles taking people to prison, but none to remove the corpse of the innocent young boy.

Death was horrific. But tyranny was even more horrific and dreadful. Khalid began crying. His mother ran to console him; she knew from her husband about the boy bleeding to death in the street. Khalid asked why the boy had been beaten up. She replied that he must have done something naughty. In school one is caned for being naughty and no blood pours out, he protested tearfully. "The cane must have hit him really hard," the mother said. "Then the boy's father should go and scold the teacher," Khalid exclaimed. "The boy's teacher is a very big man," his mother replied. "Bigger than God?" he asked. "No," she said, "not bigger than God." "In that case,"

Khalid asserted, "the boy's father should complain to God." Before going to sleep that night, he prayed to God to punish the teacher for beating up the boy, and to take away the cane that had caused so much blood to flow. Khalid had not learned his tables and was afraid that his teacher might use the same cane to punish him. "If you don't listen to me, O God," he pleaded, "I won't speak with you."[21]

Manto published his first original story under a pseudonym to avoid detection by the colonial state's intelligence services. It was a necessary precaution so soon after the uproar over the *Vera* posters that had almost landed Saadat and Hasan Abbas with a punishing jail sentence. After a fortnight an unrepentant Bari returned to Amritsar to announce the launch of *Khalq*. The first issue carried "Tamasha," a story on labor by Abu Saeed, and an essay by Bari on Hegel and Marx. Expecting trouble, Bari handed over the copies of the second issue to Manto and vanished. The secret police came looking for Bari at Manto's ancestral home in Amritsar's Lawyers' Colony. Once again one of Manto's relatives, a retired teacher with connections in the Punjab police, persuaded them that there was nothing subversive in Bari's essay, as the author had yet to grasp the philosophy of either Hegel or Marx.[22]

Bari's young disciples had no appetite for Marx or Engels. The love of materialism weighed too heavily on their gentle souls, and their individuality could not come to terms with collectivism. Bari may not have been a literary wizard, but he could tell the difference between good and bad literature. Abu Saeed recalls how Bari's tutelage made them stand out from the rest of the students at the Muslim Anglo-Oriental High School, which in 1933 acquired the status of a college. Even the professors, who included such eminent members of the progressive movement in literature as the poet Faiz Ahmad Faiz and the writer Sahibzada Mahmud-ul-Zafar, viewed their extracurricular literary activities with respect. While failing to pass the college entrance exam, Saadat, Hasan Abbas, and Abu Saeed established an Islamic Cultural Association and launched a literary journal called *Hilal*. The three were simultaneously hard at work in Saadat's room preparing an anthology of Russian literature for the literary journal *Alamgir*, published from Lahore. Under Bari's watchful eye, the young men cut no corners. They read critical works on Russian literature to facilitate the translations, and they thoroughly researched and documented the life and history of the authors and their world. They repeated the process with an anthology of French literature in Urdu translation for which the Lahore-based journal *Humayun* was selected as the medium of dissemination. By the end of his immersion in French literature, Manto pronounced Maupassant the "god of storytelling."[23]

These positive developments in Saadat's life unfolded despite ongoing financial hardships and a bout of poor health. He felt acute pain in his chest, and doctors suspected tuberculosis. To cope with it, he started consuming the harsh local whiskey and hid the bottle in a niche covered by a calendar just above his father's portrait. It was almost as if he wanted to preclude his father's severe gaze catching him in the act. Disapproving relatives, who dismissed him as cursed and degenerate, regularly reinforced the stigma of disobedience to his father. The reassuring presence of Bhagat Singh, his heartwarming smile beaming from the mantelpiece in Dar-ul-Ahmar, provided the rebel in Saadat with consolation and hope. His discovery of Abdul Bari, a veritable Don Quixote when it came to dreaming up revolutionary ideas, was

5
Manto's sister,
Nasira Iqbal,
by Saadat Hasan
Manto, ca. 1934.
Courtesy Farida
Naeem

transformative. Saadat did not know whether his guide ever claimed "Manto to be his creation," but the truth was that "he put me on the path of writing." If the two had not met, Saadat feared he might have died unknown or ended up serving a prison sentence for some robbery.[24]

Bari's success in influencing a wayward young man to embark on a literary career is remarkable. Yet in a sense the groundwork had been laid much earlier. Two individuals, both women, encouraged Saadat's penchant for storytelling—his mother, whom he called Bibijan, and his elder sister Iqbal, whose flair for telling captivating yarns in simple but sophisticated Urdu has remained one of the better-kept family secrets. Manto's frail health and impetuosity caused acute consternation for his mother and sister, both of whom responded by massaging his ego in the hope of restoring his faith in his creative abilities. Their difficulties mounted when his mother arranged Iqbal's marriage to Mohammad Umar Khan, a Pathan employee of Northwestern Railways based in Bombay. Protective of his sister, Saadat traveled to the port city to see his prospective brother-in-law's home. On returning to Amritsar, he told his mother he suspected that Khan was prone to womanizing. Instead of heeding the warning, Sardar Begum accepted the proposal, imprudently spending the bulk of her husband's meager savings on the daughter's wedding and naively handing the rest to a less-than-gracious son-in-law. Household finances now had to be met with the paltry sum of forty rupees per month, sent by two of her stepsons, while her own son seemed to be wasting his life on the streets of Amritsar dreaming of revolution. The monetary strains on his mother, coupled with his own inability to augment household finances, affected Manto deeply and exacerbated his hypersensitivity and erratic behavior.

In a letter dated 20 February 1934, to his sister in Bombay, he wrote of his mental anguish, standing at the crossroads of life, with no support, in a nondescript corner of Amritsar. He was piqued at his sister for not replying to a previous letter, and feared he might lose his mental balance if she forgot about him so soon after her marriage. Apart from their mother, his sister, whom he referred to as Balaji, was the only emotional capital he possessed. He longed for a few words from her acknowledging his existence, if only for the sake of the mutual affection they had shared as children playing on their mother's lap.[25] "Balaji, your brother may be uncultured, worthless, and peevish, but he possesses a sensitive heart filled with love, a love that is hidden but which makes the smallest oversight seem like a major event." "Nature has bestowed this weakness upon me," Manto continued, "and I cannot be blamed for it." The melodramatic letter, its tone bordering on childishness, reveals a very special bond between the two siblings. It was one that extended to a shared interest in literature. Manto clearly thought well of his sister's understanding of literature and sought her approval on every aspect of his literary endeavors. He enclosed for her perusal a copy of the college magazine he had started with Hasan Abbas at M.A.O. College, and wrote excitedly of the keen interest publishers of established literary journals were taking in his translations of Russian and French literature. In a fleeting hint of his sister's literary inklings, Manto mentions an essay of hers that he was going to submit to a magazine called *Nairang-i-Khayal*, literally, new-age thinking.[26]

Nothing is known of Nasira Iqbal's writings, though family members recall her telling delightful stories to children decades later. As her grandniece I had the privilege of hearing many exquisitely crafted stories, narrations that sometimes spanned several days. I called her Dadijan—literally, grandmother—the only person for whom I ever used the term. Whatever literary ambitions she may have nurtured ended with her marriage to a sullen and difficult man. There were agonizing disruptions that tested the relationship between the brother and the sister to the hilt. Feeling bereft and alone, Saadat underwent multiple psychological traumas

6

Manto with Abu Saeed Qureshi
on his right and fellow students
at Aligarh University, 1934

soon after his sister moved to Bombay with her husband. He
had long felt affection for a poor but nice-looking relative
called Hameeda, who, to his dismay, was married off to one
of his wealthier cousins. The disappointment only served to
magnify the inner restlessness that appeared imperceptibly

to consume the young Saadat Hasan and to account for his apparently carefree attitude toward life.

In July 1934 he failed the college entrance exams yet again. A brainwave led him and Abu Saeed to enroll in Aligarh University, for no apparent reason other than the fact that it was their intellectual mentor's alma mater. Manto's stay at Aligarh was short-lived. When he arrived by train in Aligarh, one of the sherwani-clad seniors meeting him and Abu Saeed asked whether he was related to Lord Minto (viceroy of India from 1905 to 1910). "He was my grandfather," Saadat replied, and the railway platform exploded into peals of laughter. The two young men were given accommodation in 14-SS East, which, they were told, had been the lodging of the well-known journalist and political activist Mohammad Ali Jauhar.[27] Saadat Hasan made several acquaintances at Aligarh with whom he later crossed paths. These included the progressive Urdu poet Ali Sardar Jafri, who acknowledged that Manto gave him articles on Bhagat Singh and his first introduction to Victor Hugo and Maxim Gorky.[28] Although they met a range of interesting people, neither Manto nor Abu Saeed could cope with the disciplinary regime in place at Aligarh. The university's gated solid-walled structure felt like a fortress prison where students were deprived of the elementary pleasures of elegance and beauty.[29]

From a literary perspective, Manto's brief stint at Aligarh is noteworthy for the short story "Inqilab Pasand" (Revolutionary) he wrote there in March 1935. The story was printed in the Aligarh magazine and subsequently published in 1936, along with "Tamasha," in his first-ever anthology, *Aatish Parey* (Sparks), which he dedicated to his father. Semiautobiographical, it is a story narrated by Abbas, a close friend of twenty-year-old Salim, who repeatedly fails his college entrance exams despite being intelligent. The failures are mistakenly attributed to Salim's intellectual ineptitude and vagrant behavior. In fact he is quite capable of passing the exams with the best marks in the entire province. It is just that he cannot bring himself to pay any attention to his studies. Salim takes part in all the sports played in school and is extremely popular among the boys. Everything changes for him with the unexpected death of his father. Salim is drowned in sadness. He no longer plays games; instead he spends his time deep in thought. Abbas is at a loss to understand what is going on in his friend's mind, but cannot help noticing the marked change in his behavior. Salim starts reading voluminous books by international authors and staying away from home for several days at a time. Soon he has thrown out the carefully collected posters of film stars adorning his room, along with most of the furniture, preferring to sit on the floor to read and write. One day Abbas finally asks Salim what is going on. "You know I am a revolutionary," Salim answers in all seriousness. From an initial state of disbelief, Abbas comes to realize that Salim is indeed a revolutionary, but not of the kind who believes in overthrowing the government or exploding bombs in city squares. Salim wants a revolution in everything, a transformation signified by the constantly changing face of his increasingly barren room.

The only revolution that actually transpires is the new-found clarity in Salim's perception of the world. He has seen through its injustices, hypocrisies, and lies. He begins spouting revolutionary rhetoric in public. The street children call him mad, and most people think he has taken leave of his

peeping into her heart. The experience moved Manto, inspiring him to write stories like "Misri ki Dali" (Lump of Sugar), "Beego," "Laltain" (Lantern), and a semiautobiographical piece, "Ek Khat" (A Letter), in which he refuted the impression held by some of his friends that he had spent his time in Batote dishonoring a young Kashmiri village girl. Nothing of that sort happened. He left the mountainous village teary eyed. For years afterwards he could not forget the Kashmiri girl, wondering if she had sparked in him a lifelong quest for the ineffable. The piece ended tellingly with the statement "You don't understand; nor do these people understand, why I write stories. I will tell you another time."[31] He never did so explicitly, but left plentiful clues in his stories for historians to identify, gather, and dissect.

On returning to Amritsar, Saadat was shattered to learn that his sister had lost her firstborn, a son, a crushing blow that further strained her marriage. Recalling his emotional and mental torment at the time, Manto confessed that if he had been stronger willed, he would almost certainly have committed suicide. Seeking gainful employment finally seemed like the easier option. He left for Lahore, where he got a job at the newspaper *Paras* (Philosopher's Stone), owned by Karam Chand, for forty rupees a month. The arrangement did not last long, as Manto refused to comply with the proprietor's practice of yellow journalism.[32] Restless and anxious to prove his worth, he needed a break before the financial crunch broke him to pieces. Even the presence in Lahore of his best friends, Hasan Abbas and Abu Saeed, and their guru, Bari, failed to resolve Manto's ongoing struggle to find his true vocation. The heady days spent dreaming of revolution, in the safety of Dar-ul-Ahmar in Amritsar, that

3

Bombay: Challenges and Opportunities

In the fall of 1936 Saadat Hasan moved to Bombay to take up the job of editor for the film weekly *Musawwir* (Painter), owned by Nazir Ahmad Ludhianvi. The salary was a measly forty rupees a month, exactly what he was earning in Lahore. But the prospect of living in Bombay's dynamic megalopolis excited his imagination. Saadat had high hopes for his future as a writer. India's sprawling port city and film capital offered a welter of opportunities to a talent awaiting recognition. He admitted that, like any ordinary college student, he was possessed with the desire to enter the film world. "To fulfill this passion," Manto wrote, "I had to struggle very hard."[33] Ludhianvi helped launch his film career by getting him jobs at the Imperial Film Company and Film City. The challenges and opportunities afforded by Bombay, a fast-growing city teaming with immigrants, plush with money and the amenities of modern life, was to bring out the best in Manto and leave an indelible mark on both his personality and his writings.[34]

Departing from Amritsar, he had left his mother to fend for herself. In a series of letters written to him over the next several months, she gave full expression to the love she felt for her son, and went to considerable lengths to boost his morale. Bibijan read his stories with rapt enthusiasm, recording her approval where she felt it was due, and actively engaging with their plots and characters in detail. She saw her son's imprint everywhere in *Musawwir*, since no one in Bombay, she was certain, could write the kind of quality Urdu that was being used in the journal. In a typically supportive letter, laden with prayers and advice, she wrote:

> Saadat, may God give you a long life, by God's grace you are very clever and promising. If you do not let effort and tenacity slip out of your hands, by God's grace you will soon be successful. . . . Steer away from contention and vice, and, my darling son, God will shower you with His blessings. . . . may you shine forth and be respected in every corner of the world, and be worthy of praise and appreciation and may God keep you free from dependence on anyone.[35]

Manto's spirits were lifted by his mother's keen appreciation of his early stories and unflinching belief in his impending success. Practically, life in Bombay was difficult. He was earning a pittance and paying rent for the privilege of camping at *Musawwir*'s office. A spendthrift who loved buying books more than eating food, he was excessively generous toward friends and acquaintances. Whatever little was left of his modest salary, he burned up on drink, expensive fountain pens, and his fetish for shoes, which he liked collecting and giving away as presents to friends and relatives.[36]

Soon after his arrival, there were Hindu-Muslim clashes in the city from October to early December 1936, leading to several deaths and the arrest of more than two thousand. The disturbances erupted when some Muslims took exception to the reconstruction of the Byculla Temple's assembly hall (the original structure had been demolished by the colonial authorities to make way for a road). Based on the flimsy logic that the construction would disturb intercommunitarian relations, the objection was intrusive and designed to foment trouble. Some influential Muslim leaders tried involving Mohammad Ali Jinnah, the prominent barrister and leader of the All-India Muslim League, to work out a compromise. Unwilling to concede an inch of their turf, local ulema sabotaged the attempt and issued eight conflicting fatwas instructing their followers to protest the playing of music before the mosque in the vicinity of the Byculla Temple.[37] Local Hindus retaliated with fury, plunging the city into chaos. Shocked by the mayhem and bloodshed he had witnessed, Manto penned a tearful and stirring appeal to the residents of the city. The substance of his plea was that the merciless killing of fellow human beings was abhorrent to all reasonable individuals except those with a criminal bent. He condemned the savagery and pointed an accusing finger at self-serving leaders who, devoid of faith and ethics, made a mockery of religion with their thunderous and insincere sermons. These so-called leaders, who used communitarian violence to further their own purposes, were not only a blot on the face of humanity, they were pulling India off the road to freedom into a dark and deep abyss. They had to be identified and their malevolent deeds exposed.[38]

"Saadat, I liked your appeal very much," Bibijan wrote, appreciating his "impassioned attempt at awakening the country and the nation to stop the recent spate of violence." According to her, it was the first appeal of its kind in India to fervently call for the cessation of hostilities between the two communities. She commended him for his courage in uncovering the nefarious intentions of the rabble-rousers. He had done the Bombayites a great favor with his timely, well-crafted, and thoughtful appeal, exhorting Hindus and Muslims to forge a united front. His principled line of argument and respect for both religion and nation would help lay the basis for a unified nationality. If all patriots and supporters of Hindu-Muslim cooperation accepted the appeal, the bigotry and mutual misunderstandings between the two communities would soon disappear. The people of Bombay, especially the educated ones, needed to come out openly in support of him. Otherwise the communitarian tensions enveloping the city could make his high-minded ideas seem like a deliberate provocation. Bibijan regretted that he had mentioned the ringleader of the troublemakers by name. Making enemies was not a wise thing to do.[39]

She was right. The only known reaction to the appeal came from Muslim goons, at whose hands Manto narrowly escaped being roughed up. In sticking his neck out for an issue few others had dared to address publicly, the newcomer to cosmopolitan Bombay had opened his account as a staunch proponent of a civic nationalism devoid of petty identity politics in the name of religion. Uninterested in the twists and turns of Indian politics of any variety, Manto was nevertheless an astute observer of the human condition. He knew better than anyone that most politicians—not unlike the prostitutes he took to writing about, as a metaphor for the constant exchange of commodities in the bazaar—were forever transacting business in which morality and ethics played a marginal role at best. Nothing irked him more than people whose moralizing ig-

7
Manto in Bombay

nored the elementary rules of human decency. So while taking note of his mother's sound advice to avoid making enemies, Manto was not prepared to compromise his beliefs for the sake of congeniality with those he considered insincere and disdainfully characterized as "frauds."

His temperamental aversion to sanctimonious hypocrisy did not help open doors in an unfamiliar metropolis, delaying the realization of his mother's dream, a vision of him at the pinnacle of success as a writer and intellectual. After gaining employment in Film City, Manto left *Musawwir*'s office and took up residence in a filthy, bug-infested hovel. His mother, who had just moved away from Amritsar to live with her daughter, wept profusely upon seeing the dismal conditions in which he was living. By then Manto had fallen out with his brother-in-law and was prohibited from meeting the sister to whom he was so attached. The special bond between the two siblings survived the artificially enforced separation, which came to an end only after the death of Balaji's husband in 1948. Despite the constraints on her, she facilitated her mother's efforts to arrange Saadat's marriage into a respectable middle-class Kashmiri family. Unable to attend the wedding, Iqbal asked Manto to stop outside her home, which was a minute away from the bride's home in Mahim, so that she could see him dressed as a groom. They had a short and emotional meeting on the footpath leading to his in-laws' residence.[40] Balaji also continued informing his literary career in spirit. Manto's renowned ability to pierce the inner recesses of women's hearts and minds owed something to her knack for passing on offbeat and captivating anecdotes and stories she had heard from her girlfriends and acquaintances.

Safia, whom he married on 26 April 1939, was the other woman who provided Manto with rare insights into the female psyche that might have eluded him if he had relied on the art of observation alone. She had grown up in East Africa, where her father, Khwaja Qamaruddin, was a public prosecutor in the Zanzibar police. Her mother, Miraj Begum, had moved back to Bombay with her three daughters and two younger sons—the elder two stayed behind in East Africa—after Qamaruddin was killed in a clash between the British and local Arab insurgents, who mistook him for an Englishman because of his very fair complexion. Since Saadat's two elder brothers also had connections with East Africa, Bibijan and Iqbal were quickly able to establish contact with Safia's

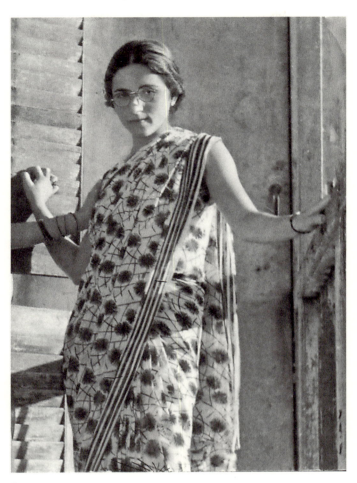

8

Manto's wife, Safia.

Courtesy Nighat Patel

family. Manto agreed to the arrangement without seeing Safia, which was not untypical at the time. He once lightheartedly described all that he shared in common with his future wife, proudly highlighting the fact that, like him, she belonged to a Kashmiri family:

> Her father is dead. My father is also not alive. She wears glasses; I wear glasses. She was born on 11 May and I too was born on 11 May. Her mother wears glasses. My mother wears glasses as well. The first letter in her name is "S." The first letter in my name is also "S." We have all these things in common. The rest I am as yet unaware of. Previously she did not observe purdah, but ever since I have acquired a right over her she has been observing purdah (only from me).[41]

Manto's relatively conservative personal life did not limit his literary vision. Enough had been written about devoted and pious-hearted wives. Such stories were now useless. "Why not reveal the heart of a woman who leaves her husband for another man's embrace while the husband sits in the same room watching as if nothing is happening?" In his opinion, "life ought to be presented as it is, not as it was or as it will be or should be."[42]

Saadat Hasan's evolution from an imaginative prankster, who dared to walk on burning coals as a youngster in Amritsar, into a leading writer of Urdu short stories and film scripts was neither coincidental nor accidental.[43] A freethinker by choice and design, Manto authored his own personality and acknowledged no literary influence on his work. The only individual for whom he showed deference, and of whom he confessed to being in complete awe, was the outstanding Persian and Urdu poet Mirza Asadullah Khan Ghalib. A shared affinity with Ghalib, who also had to struggle to make a living despite his prodigious talent, was only natural. Manto once said that there was no point in composing poetry in Urdu after Ghalib. He was not as generous toward others. "I have had the opportunity to read innumerable Western and Eastern authors, but there is no book that has satisfied my aesthetic sensibility." This was not sheer arrogance. He confessed that while some of his admirers ranked him among the leading authors of the day, he himself had never been satisfied with any of the stories, dramas, or essays he had written. In fact, he had not even come within sight of the destination he had in mind for himself. The truth was that during his school years he had cared nothing for the subtleties of Urdu. He had remained unfamiliar with the sweetness of its diction, which had made it so popular within a short span of time that it was the third most widely spoken language in the world. But he had since made up for these weaknesses through extensive study of the language and its literature. People called him crazy, shallow, and obdurate, but he paid no heed and remained a bookworm until he felt that his literary endeavors could withstand criticism. Manto realized that he had to devote the rest of his life to his art if he was to attain the quality of writing that would satisfy his aspirations.[44] In another rare moment of humility, he said that he wrote because he had to feed himself: "Saadat Hasan Manto writes because he is not as great a storyteller and poet as God. It is his lowliness that makes him write."[45]

What Manto wrote about, however, attests to his role as a witness to history, a chronicler of exceptional perception, foresight, and skepticism. His personal honesty and intensity of observation enabled him to understand people's psyches and their situations, to tell some plain and awkward truths. "As a human being I have many weaknesses," he conceded. "I always fear that they may create hatred for me among others,

Civil War, having overheard the news at the local fair. Ustad Mangu's geography, however, is weak. Asked where Spain is, he says, "In Vilayat [England], where else." But he needs no lofty lessons in nationalism. He hates the British for keeping India subjugated and allowing their soldiers—tommies, as they were called—to humiliate and ill-treat him and his countrymen. He has a novel explanation for the recurrence of Hindu-Muslim clashes. According to his elders, the emperor Akbar had once displeased a dervish, who put a curse on the kingdom. This is why Hindus and Muslims are forever at each other's throats, and the reason Hindustan can never be free of foreign rule, regardless of what the Congress wants. One day, Ustad Mangu overhears that India is to have a new constitution and will become independent on the first of April. He is delighted. The more he hears about the impending changes under the new constitution, the more Ustad Mangu becomes convinced that a shining new era is about to dawn.

On 1 April 1935 he prepares his tonga early in the morning and sets out to witness the effects of the new constitution. Mangu leaps at the opportunity to drive a fare to the Cantonment, where the obnoxious British soldiers he so loathes are stationed. After dropping off the passenger, he starts daydreaming about the new constitution. While his pony is slowly trudging down the road, he spots a tommy standing near a lamppost signaling at him. Mangu looks at him disdainfully. His contempt grows when he realizes that this is the same soldier with whom he had an altercation a year ago. The tommy had been drunk and abused Mangu, who restrained himself, as magistrates dealt severely with poor tonga drivers. Things are different now, he thinks. So when the tommy asks how much he would charge for a trip to the Hira Mandi, Lahore's red-light district, Mangu quotes a price of five rupees, much more than the normal fare. "Are you mad?," the tommy shouts indignantly. Then, recalling their spat the previous year, the solider imperiously points his baton at the burly tonga driver and orders him to step down from the carriage. A fist lands on the tommy's chin, as Mangu begins beating him black-and-blue, saying: "Still the same high-and-mighty tone . . . it's the first of April and now we are our own masters." People gather to watch the spectacle. It takes two policemen to extricate the soldier from Mangu, who is panting for breath and foaming at the mouth, yelling, "Gone are the days of the British . . . we now have a new constitution, brothers . . . a new constitution." "What new laws and what rights are you shouting about?" he is asked at the police station; "the laws are the same old ones"—and then Mangu is unceremoniously tossed into prison.[49]

"Naya Qanun" was published in *Humayun* in May 1938 and widely hailed in literary circles for its simple and effective narrative. It established Manto's reputation as a skillful observer of the human psyche. As always, Mangu's character was based on a real live person—tonga drivers had their own union in Lahore. Manto's perspicacity and uncanny prescience were revealed when, on 1 August 1945, the *Hindu* of Madras published a news item about a Lahore tonga driver who, excited by the victory of the Labour Party in Britain, assaulted a police constable with his whip after being hauled up for infringing traffic rules. "Don't you know that comrade Attlee is in power?" the tonga driver howled at the shocked and bruised constable. "You will have to behave yourself well."[50]

By the time "Naya Qanun" was being talked about in literary circles, Manto had become formally betrothed to Safia.

9
Saadat Hasan and Safia Manto,
by Brij Mohan, Bombay, 1947

The actual wedding had not taken place owing to his uncertain finances. Although his health remained indifferent, he
showed an enterprising streak during this period. Shooting for
his story *Mujhe Paapi Kaho*—literally, call me a sinner—was
being completed at the Imperial Film Company. Attracted
by the well-paid opportunities available in the Bombay film
industry, he started concentrating on scripts like *Keechar*
(Mud), which Manto completed with the collaboration of
the famous Urdu and Hindi short story writer Krishan Chander (1914–1977). The film version was called *Apni Nagariya*

(Own Place). It was released on 26 January 1940; the story was substantially amended, to Manto's chagrin, but the film did well at the box office. He contemplated a film script called *Parosi* (Neighbors) on the question of Hindu-Muslim unity, which he wanted to bring to the screen in all its intricate dimensions. Since the mosque-temple issue was a barrier to that unity, he intended to foreground the home of a prostitute as the common meeting point of the two communities.[51] Despite Manto's innovative ideas and the quality of his writing, remuneration for his efforts was invariably delayed. Some directors, if they liked his stories, often found his dialogues difficult to grasp. The films for which he wrote the scripts were rarely box office successes. To make ends meet, he wrote plays, stories, sketches, and literary reviews for All-India Radio Bombay and even tried starting a news agency with a view to selling interesting stories internationally. The frenetic pace of his life in those days led him to quip that he was like "a kebab full of ants."[52]

Marrying Safia brought happiness but also increased his financial woes. He complained of having no spare time. His life was like a speeding train passing through town after town, but he was so exhausted and fed up at the very outset of the journey that he could not read the names of the stations posted on the signboards. He could not quite grasp his strange condition—indeed, how could he, since there was no time to spend on understanding what was going on.[53] Manto's agitated state was no barrier to his creativity, and he wrote several short stories, film scripts, and radio plays. Looking to augment his sources of income, he published short stories like "Hameed aur Hameeda" under Safia's name—an indication that their companionship now extended into the literary realm. But his newfound happiness was cut short by the sudden loss of his mother in June 1940. Manto was shattered. He fell ill and went into a depression that was only partially offset by the distractions afforded by his firstborn, a son named Arif, whom he pampered to a fault. To mitigate his mounting physical, psychological, and monetary troubles, and also to provide support for Safia in taking care of Arif, Manto moved in with his in-laws at 12 Mohammad Jaffar House on Lady Jamshedji Road in Mahim.

The change of residence coincided with Manto's losing his job at *Musawwir*, a crushing blow to his sense of self. The termination notice handed to him by his friend and fellow employee, Agha Khalash Kashmiri, stung Manto. Neither Ludhianvi, nor the paper's patron, Kirpa Ram, gave any explanation for the abrupt dismissal. He had always relied on these two to get jobs. The film positions Ludhianvi had secured for him were now taken away. A comfortable monthly salary of 120 rupees was suddenly snatched away from him for an unnamed offense. Manto was livid. He took a job on half the salary as editor of Baburao Patel's gossipy film weekly *Caravan*. Shortly afterwards he met Kirpa Ram, who blandly said: "I expected you and Safia to come and see me as soon as you received the termination notice; we would have worked out some reconciliation. But you did not come and went to Baburao Patel instead." Deeply affronted, Manto thundered: "Bless the pandit's honor, maybe he does not know people who do not beg even after losing 120 rupees." Kirpa Ram's words, Manto was convinced, would resonate in his mind even on his deathbed. Feeling used and abused by Ludhianvi and Kirpa Ram, who made him write critically about people whom they simultaneously rubbed shoulders with, Manto confessed that if he had not been married, suicide would have been his preferred option. It was better to die than live a lowly life, begging others for favors just to earn money to survive.[54]

While he managed to pick himself up to write several short stories and embark on promising new projects, including a screenplay on the life of his literary hero, Ghalib, Manto had hit a wall with his career in Bombay. So he decided to throw in the towel and take up a semiofficial job at All-India Radio in New Delhi. This phase in his life was to give a new dimension to Manto's cosmopolitan outlook. His move to India's capital city brought both happiness and tears. A steady salary meant peace of mind, even as New Delhi's climate led to a distinct improvement in his health. He initially lived with his family at 6 Sadiq Manzil, Nicholson Road, before moving to flat number 9 in Hasan Building, on the same road, near Kashmiri Gate. Manto was crazy about his son and attended to all his needs with exacting care. Tragically the boy died on, 28 April 1941, of pneumonia. Manto was devastated and inconsolable.

The struggle to eke out a living forced him to keep going. He made new friends as well as enemies, and came to accept a new category of enemy friends—"frenemies," in today's parlance. When an enemy friend intrigued to get one of Manto's radio dramas revised, he picked up his typewriter and quit All-India Radio, where he had written about a hundred plays over a period of one and a half years.[55] It was an act of defiance he could ill afford, given his precarious financial state. In 1942 one of Manto's short stories, "Kali Shalwar," published in the annual number of *Adab-i-Latif* (Lahore), was banned by the colonial state under section 292 of the Indian Penal Code on grounds of obscenity. Under the law only the editor, printer, and publisher could be charged; thus the case was dismissed after an appeal was filed. Manto was to be booked for obscenity on four more occasions, two in British India and another two in postcolonial Pakistan. Defending himself against the initial charge of obscenity, he maintained that storytelling was as old as Adam and would last until the end of time. It had once found form in revelatory texts attributed to prophets. Now that there was no scope for prophets, stories appeared in newspapers, journals, and books. "I am a human being who writes in these journals and books, and I write because I have something to say." "Whatever I see and from whatever perspective," Manto continued, "I present that same perspective to others." If all those who wrote were mad, he was happy to be included among them. His story was about an ordinary prostitute who worked for a living. "If one could talk about temples and mosques, then why could one not talk about whorehouses from where many people went to temples and mosques?"[56]

On 7 August 1942, when Manto returned to Bombay to resume his work as editor of *Musawwir*, the office phone line was dead. Anticipating the passage of the Quit India resolution the following day, the colonial state's coercive machinery had started arresting the top Congress leadership, including Mohandas Gandhi, Jawaharlal Nehru, and Abul Kalam Azad. The severity of the crackdown was a result of British anxieties about Japan's military successes in Southeast Asia. The fall of Singapore to the Japanese in February 1942 shattered confidence in British invincibility. To alleviate the blow, the American president Franklin D. Roosevelt prevailed upon Prime Minister Winston Churchill to make some sort of a gesture to win the cooperation of the Indian nationalist leadership in the war against the Japanese. The failure of the mission headed by the Labour leader, Sir Stafford Cripps, in the spring of 1942 prompted Gandhi to draft a resolution calling on the British to quit India. In the Mahatma's characteristically canny view, the Japanese would have no reason to invade if the British were no longer in India. Gandhi was ready to risk violence to end "the greater calamity of slavery," because "ordered anarchy" was "worse than real anarchy."[57] Heeding Gandhi's slogan "Do or die," students and workers joined the second tier of Congress activists to call on the colonial masters to quit India. Rattled by the strength of the protests, the British were swift and brutal in cracking down.

Unbeknown to Manto, his life and work from now on were to become imperceptibly interwoven in the broader canvas of politics that he neither quite understood nor took much interest in. Safia was by his side a few days later. Finances were not too bad, since he was able to sell a film script called *Naukar* (Servant). He stayed home writing stories until 26 July 1943, when he sold *Ghar ki Shobha* (Beauty of the Home) for the handsome sum of 1,250 rupees.[58] Dissatisfied with the quality of his output since returning to Bombay, Manto maintained that he had not concentrated on anything long enough to produce something worthwhile. "I have started drinking a lot," he told his friend and fellow writer Ahmad Nadeem Qasimi, "not so that I can write—I cannot write when I have been drinking—but actually to find that something within me that I have to do." Feeling unfulfilled by his work, Manto wrote: "If I have to just do what I have been doing until now, then it is a mere travesty and no great achievement at all."[59]

These were the words of an author who was already being referred to as the father of the Urdu short story and a "unique literary miracle" destined for immortality.[60] Manto had always set his sights much higher than anyone else. But even his literary vision could not have framed, far less wished for, what was to come. The dramatic turn of events in India would afford extraordinary opportunities to a short story writer who, much like a historian, wanted to capture something unusual, unseen, but meaningful about life as it is, and not as it is supposed to be. In a stark comment on the unreasonableness of all-India politics, Manto in 1945 crafted a shocking story called "Mootri" (Urinal). Located not far from Congress House and Jinnah Hall in Bombay, the urinal stank to high heaven, making it impossible for anyone to walk past it without covering his nose with a handkerchief. Filthy beyond belief, its walls were covered with unspeakable visual and verbal obscenities that intensified the stench. The centerpiece was the phrase "shoved Pakistan up the Muslim sister's . . ." After a few days, a response appeared on the wall, written with a thick pencil: "shoved united India up the Hindu mother's . . ." More time passed. Gandhi was released from prison unconditionally, while Jinnah suffered a setback in Punjab. Congress House and Jinnah Hall stayed under government control, neither defeated nor released. The urinal a few yards away remained captive to foul-smelling odors. But its walls exemplified free speech of a profound kind. One day a new response adorned the urinal's wall where the earlier two statements had faded: "shoved Mother India up both Hindus and Muslims." For a moment, but only fleetingly, the stink dispelled and a subtle fragrance wafted through the house of fetor.[61]

With his strong sense of empathy and his ability to get down to the bone of things, Manto's partition-related stories do not pass judgment on events or human actions but seek to tease out their inwardness. He knew that one could commit the same mistakes as someone else. In his opinion, the fault is not that of the person making the mistake; rather, it lies in the nature of circumstances in whose fields man sows and reaps the fruits. Manto had started his literary itinerary with "Tamasha"; his "1919 ki aik Baat" (A Story of 1919), written after partition, underlines his belief in the interconnectedness of events that preceded the brutal vivisection of the subcontinent. Partition on this view was not a disjuncture but an intimate aspect of the inner dynamics of India's history.

Translated into English in *Black Milk* as "Thalia the Pimp," "A Story of 1919" was written between 11 and 12 October 1951 in Manto's new home at 31 Lakshmi Mansions, Lahore. Based on events leading up to the Jallianwalla Bagh massacre, the story revolves around Muhammad Tufail, pejoratively known as Thalia "kanjir"—literally, pimp—though he has never been in the business of procuring women for anyone. Handsome, well-dressed, and witty, he is the good-for-nothing son of a rich prostitute who lives in Amritsar's red-light district. With plenty of money at his disposal he took to wine, women, and gambling at a tender age. Thalia's debauched lifestyle has made him the object of disdain in the Prostitutes' Bazaar. Even his own sisters, Shamshad and Almas, both of whom are prostitutes and the pride of the profession, have disowned him. When the troubles start, the British react with excessive force, inflaming tempers beyond control. An unarmed procession protesting Gandhi's arrest in Lahore and restrictions on their local leaders is fired upon by a group of British soldiers guarding the Railway Bridge leading to the Civil Lines, the residential area for district officers and lackeys of the colonial state. Several protesters are wounded and some trampled underfoot in the stampede.

Thalia is standing some sixty or seventy yards away with a group of excited young men, who are venting their anger at the indiscriminate shooting by throwing stones at the big clock crowning Hall Gate, an elegant structure in the heart of Amristar city harking back to the Mughal era. After the dial has been smashed to smithereens, one of them shouts, "Let's smash the Queen's statue." Someone suggests setting the town hall on fire. "Stop," Thalia shouts, "what good will that do? Let's go to the Bridge and wipe out the tommies." Nobody pays him any heed, and the group proceeds toward the statue. Thalia exhorts them not to waste their energies: "Let's go for the tommies, the murderers of our innocent countrymen." Only a few follow Thalia as he heads toward the bridge. As he reaches the bridge's railing, the soldiers open fire. Undeterred, Thalia keeps advancing despite being shot in the chest, his sparkling white silk shirt turning ruby red as he leaps at one of the tommies on a horse and pulls him to the ground. There is a hail of gunfire, but Thalia has made his point. He is found with his fingers so deeply clawed into the throat of the dead British soldier that it takes considerable effort to separate the two bodies. The killing of their own countrymen, more than the looting of banks and the demolition of statues, contributes to the colonial rage that leads to the unconscionable massacre at Jallianwalla Bagh.

Thalia has been far from perfect. But when his bullet-riddled body is carried to the Prostitutes' Bazaar, all the denizens beat their breasts and weep aloud. His sisters faint and shed tears of blood when his bier is lifted for the final journey. Martial law has been declared in the city, and so Thalia has to be buried in secret without ceremony, almost as if his death were a crime committed by his bereaved family. His name does not appear on the list of people martyred by the British in the Punjab bloodbath. Nor are the sacrifices of his two sisters counted among the honorable deeds performed during the anticolonial struggle. Their story is quite as gripping as Thalia's. Upon hearing from their Indian informers of the rare beauty and singing talents of the pimp's two sisters, the British army officers decide to send for them, with a view to using the opportunity to both humiliate them and avenge the death of Miss Sherwood, an Englishwoman who has perished in the disturbances. Thalia's grave is still fresh when his sisters receive the summons. Yet they go fully made up and perform before the inebriated British officers well into the night. When the merrymaking comes to an end, the two women tear off their clothes and stand naked before their tormentors, screaming: "We are Thalia's sisters . . . sisters of that martyr, whose beautiful body you riddled with your bullets . . . the body that housed his freedom loving soul. . . . come and defile our scented bodies with your evil smelling passion, but before you do that, all we want is an opportunity to spit in your face." Their daring act is remembered with shame even by those well disposed to Thalia and his family. The sisters are are castigated as "shameless bitches"; they have disgraced their brother and his martyrdom.[62]

This grim story gives the lie to nationalist narratives identifying Gandhian nonviolence as the primary dynamic in the anticolonial struggle. It also exposes the hypocrisy implicit in honoring the heroics of male martyrs and stigmatizing the passive resistance of women prostitutes. Manto used his admirable command of the short narrative form not only to lay bare the hearts of his characters, whether individual men or women; he was equally adamant about forcing society collectively to look at its uglier side through the mirror of the pages he crafted with such exquisite brevity, clarity, and speed. He is among the best practitioners of partition storytelling not only because he questioned the wisdom of the rupture—as in his acclaimed stories "Toba Tek Singh," "The Last Salute," and the like—or because he wrote impartially and without malice toward any community. Manto's stories are important sources for historians because they seriously unsettle the dominant communitarian mode of analyzing partition violence. He knows how to rankle. The success of his stories about the violence unleashed by the British decision to divide and quit can be measured in direct proportion to the degree of unease felt by those accustomed to perceiving and comprehending things through the distorting prism of religious identities.

In "Tayaqqun" (An Anguished Certitude), Manto ridicules the efforts of the two newly independent states of India and Pakistan to stitch together the shreds of women's honor by rehabilitating those who were abducted during the communitarian frenzy in Punjab. The heartbreaking story revolves around a disheveled and crazed woman who is desperately searching for her daughter. The liaison officer recounting the story to the author finds the poor woman in increasingly more pathetic circumstances in different parts of Punjab. He repeatedly tells her that her daughter has been killed in Patiala, and that she should accompany him to Pakistan. But she refuses to believe that her beautiful daughter could have been killed. One day the liaison officer spots the old woman in Amritsar at the same time as he sees a young woman, draped in a white cotton chador, walking down the street with a sprightly and good-looking young Sikh. On seeing the old woman, the Sikh stops and says to the girl, "Your mother." The young woman, who is stunningly beautiful, lifts the veil, looks at her mother fleetingly, and then, grabbing the Sikh's arm, says, "Let's go," and walks away. The distraught mother calls after her daughter. The liaison officer once again tells her that her daughter is dead. The anguished woman screams: "You are lying." When the liaison officer swears on God's name that her daughter is indeed dead, the woman's certitude finally crumbles; she falls down in the square and dies. Apart from drawing attention to the irony inherent in terms like "abducted and rehabilitated women," Manto leaves the truth mystifyingly unclear: the reader never knows whether the young woman had run away with the Sikh, or, if she was kidnapped, had made her peace with him and no longer wanted to be reunited with her hapless and tragic mother.[63]

Blending hard facts with shards of realistic fiction, Manto was able to document the multifaceted nature of human sufferings at the time of partition that has eluded professional historians owing to the methodological limitations of their craft. Unfettered by the demands of communitarian narratives promoted by postcolonial states to project their national ideologies, he enters the hearts and minds of both the perpetrators and the victims of violence without compromising his sense of humanity and reasonableness. So was Manto the better historian, then, if by that term we mean someone with the ability to narrate the past in a way that stands the test of time? And was he aware of his role as witness and maker of history? From a literary perspective it is quite striking that his stories before the cataclysm of partition were far more attentive to the intricacies of language and the delicacies of form. After that debacle he wrote in simpler and more accessible language in order to make sense of the painful displacement and hor-

10
Humanity on the move—a convoy of Muslims
migrating from the Sikh state of Faridkot after
partition, by Margaret Bourke-White. Time &
Life Pictures/Getty Images

rific bloodbath that had stained the milk of human kindness a
harsh reddish black.

Manto was first introduced to the English-speaking world
in 1956 by his nephew Hamid Jalal, who translated a selection
of his short stories in a volume entitled *Black Milk*. Manto
personally scrutinized all the translations, giving them an edge

over others that were done after his death. *Black Milk* was presented to the international seminar series run by Henry Kissinger at Harvard University. The impressive collection includes the story "Parhiyae Kalima"—literally, recite the Muslim confessional, translated as "Nothing but the Truth." One of Manto's most memorable stories, it tells of a powerfully built Hindu woman, Rukma, who responds to the advances of a Muslim besotted by her, murders her husband, Girdhari, and gets the prospective lover to help dispose of the corpse. Taking advantage of the disturbed conditions prevailing in the city, and breaking the curfew, the new paramour, Abdul, throws the dead body into a garbage dump outside a mosque. Later that evening Hindu arsonists burn down the mosque, and Girdhari's body is never discovered. Abdul has a short and steamy affair with Rukma before she moves on to a new lover, Tukaram, the neighborhood fruit seller. After miraculously surviving a murderous assault by Rukma, Abdul ends up throwing her out the window. The next morning he is shocked to find that there is no sign of Rukma's body. People living in the neighborhood think that she has been either abducted by a Muslim or killed in the violence. Abdul is relieved and tells himself: "If she's been killed, then so much the better . . . but if someone has abducted her and taken her some place then we know what he's in for . . . may God protect him!"

Twenty days after Rukma's disappearance, Abdul encounters Tukaram, who asks him about her. Abdul swears by the Quran that he knows nothing. Tukaram refuses to believe this, and threatens to go to the police to report that Abdul had killed Girdhari and now Rukma. Thinking he has no choice, Abdul quietly sharpens his knife and sets out in search of Tukaram. Finding the fruit seller in the urinal, Abdul calls him by name and stabs him in his stomach. But then, instead of running away, he bends down to check Tukaram's pulse to make sure he is dead. Just then a constable enters the urinal and Abdul, sure he has been caught red-handed, foolishly blurts out a confession. But it was a crime of passion, he insists, if not an act of self-defense. He has not ripped open Tukaram's belly because he was a Hindu:

"I swear by God. . . . There is but one God and Muhammad is His Messenger . . . You are Muslims, believe what I say . . . I'll speak nothing but the truth. . . . Pakistan has nothing to do with this. . . . I can lay down my life for Quaid-i-Azam Muhammad Ali Jinnah, but I swear by God that Pakistan has nothing to do with this. . . . In the last Hindu-Muslim riots, I killed three Hindus, but believe me those killings were quite another matter. . . . I have told you the truth, nothing but the truth."[64]

II

Memories

Of Bald Angels *and "Krishna's Flute"*

Remembering Partition

At the famed midnight hour of 15 August 1947, Indians marked the end of two centuries of subjugation and humiliation at British hands. Expressions of joy tinged with anger and bitterness at the partition of the subcontinent periodically exploded in visceral rage against members of other religious communities. In Punjab at large, and Amritsar in particular, former slaves celebrated freedom by burning down the homes of their neighbors. Before anyone knew whether Amritsar would be included in India or in Pakistan, half the city had been gutted. Outside the Lawyers' Colony was a mountain of rubble, including bricks and mortar from Saadat Hasan Manto's destroyed ancestral home. Casting a nostalgic look at his hometown in October 1951, Manto started "A Story of 1919" wondering what the events of 1947 had done to Amritsar— the center of the anticolonial struggle where British machine gunners had ruthlessly mowed down hundreds of freedom lovers. He wanted to remember those glory days. "Forget about recent events," he wrote; "their memory lies heavy on my heart." Some people blamed the British for the carnage at

11
Uprooted people—a Sikh family
migrating to Indian Punjab,
by Margaret Bourke-White.
Time & Life Pictures/Getty Images

the time of partition, but Manto could not "help seeing the blood on our own hands."[1]

Recollection and forgetting are so intrinsic to the art of historical narration that disentangling the two can be a delicate and exacting exercise. There has been a near obsession with memory studies among recent scholars of traumatic events in modern history. Memory as a means of historical retrieval has its limitations. Apart from the problems inherent in selective remembering, there is memory's intrinsic and complex relationship with the knotty issue of responsibility. The issue is knottier in the case of partition violence than in that of the Holocaust. In the latter, a totalitarian state orchestrated a genocidal campaign against a community for racial and supremacist reasons. By contrast, there were perpetrators and victims of a murderous orgy in 1947 among Hindus, Muslims, and Sikhs in the midst of the abdication of all sense of responsibility by managers of a departing colonial state. A recent tendency to romanticize memory and nostalgia in antihistorical representations of the past has obscured the ways in which the manipulation of memories of trauma both reinforces and advances nationalist narratives of the postcolonial state. Even when the fracturing of national imaginaries allows memories to escape the statist imprint, personal and collective memories are rarely if ever immune from the persistence of the present in selective remembrances of the past.

Memories of partition were ritually invoked by both participants and observers describing the brutal killings of Sikhs in New Delhi in the wake of Indira Gandhi's assassination. The same memory bank was drawn upon by those attempting to come to terms with the extensive violence that swept across the subcontinent after the destruction of the Babri mosque, in December 1992, by organized gangs of volunteers affiliated with right-wing Hindu parties and their equally rabid counterparts in Pakistan and Bangladesh. Urvashi Butalia admits that her study of women's experiences during partition was motivated by "an increasingly communal presence" in India after the razing of the mosque. She commented that "descriptions of practically all communal strife" in India "hark back to it ('it was like Partition again')."[2] Attributed to religious communalism, an overarching category that obfuscates more than it reveals, these tragic incidents have been naturalized in narratives of social conflict in subcontinental conditions as periodic occurrences whose only certainty lies in their recurrence. This raises a necessary and profoundly historical question about memory that is often glossed over: have different moments of remembrance produced contrasting memories about social relations between religious communities? Pursuing this question may disturb the certitude conceded to anguished memories and spell out the extent to which partition, as an event, is "inexplicable," as is sometimes claimed, in terms of the dominant historical modes of reasoning.

Scholars of South Asia have been exposing the tendentious and limited nature of statist narratives. In recent years the personal side of the partition tragedy has become an especially popular genre of writing. While invoking the spirit of humanism, these works often end up reaffirming the equation of religious differences with conflict by ascribing the pain and suffering to an amorphous and ill-defined notion of "communal" violence. Without in any way minimizing the trauma of 1947, we must look at the other side of partition, so to speak. I am not referring to the incorporation of the marginal or the subaltern agent, which South Asian historians, anthropologists, and literary critics have been doing with varying measures of success. Looking at the other side of partition entails cutting across the communitarian morass and foregrounding the cosmopolitanism of everyday life that bound people belonging to rival religious communities both before and after the severity of a forced separation no one had quite envisaged, simply because there was no precedent for it in India's history.

A social renegade like Manto may not seem like an obvious choice for such an investigation. But his knack for plumbing the depths of the human psyche and raising ethically disturbing social questions makes him both an important resource and an intriguing case study. Manto wrote two sets of character sketches, twelve under the title *Ganjay Farishtay* (Bald Angels) and ten in a collection called *Loudspeaker*. With the exception of the sketch on Mohammad Ali Jinnah, which is based on what Jinnah's driver had related, all the other sketches portray famous personalities Manto came to know at some point in his life. After moving to Lahore in 1948, he turned to this genre of writing in large part to avoid the censor's eye and the inconveniences of defending himself against another round of obscenity charges. In the preface to *Bald Angels*, Manto declared:

> To tell the truth I was so fed up that I considered getting
> an allotment and sitting comfortably in some corner for
> a few years far away from both pen and ink and hanging
> on the gallows any thoughts occurring in my mind.

After much consideration, Manto decided to write on film stars he had known personally. It seemed to be the best way of avoiding government censorship and keeping the puritans satisfied.[3] But in his choice of characters for the sketches, Manto remained true to his interest in the offbeat and quirky aspects of life. He wrote about unconventional individuals, giving readers glimpses into their inner world as well as the less familiar aspects of their social persona. His all-too-frank and true-to-life depictions of adulated film stars and other well-known figures shocked readers, and invited brickbats from those who questioned his sense of propriety in exposing the faults of departed souls. Manto defended himself resolutely:

It is a rule in every respectable country and society in the world that the dead, even if one's enemies, are spoken of in positive terms. Only good qualities are mentioned and the bad ones kept hidden. I damn such a respectable world and society where as a rule the character of the dead is sent to a laundry for a wash and then placed on a high pedestal. In my reformatory there is no support, no shampoo, no hair-curling machine. . . . I am not a makeup artist. . . . all the angels in my book have their heads shaved, and I have performed that ritual with great finesse.[4]

This is what makes Manto's personality sketches such an excellent repository for the retrieval of memories without the bitter clouds of communitarian animosities that have made remembering partition a contentious and divisive subject.

From Cinema City to
Conquering Air Waves

During his all-too-brief life of forty-two years spanning Amritsar, Bombay, Delhi, and Lahore, Manto came into contact with many people and forged some extraordinary friendships that withstood the strains of arbitrary frontiers between India and Pakistan. His cosmopolitanism can be gleaned at one level from his keen interest in Russian, French, and Chinese literature and, on another, from his firm refusal to allow distinctions of religion to interfere with his choice of friends. His extensive galaxy of friends and acquaintances, to name just a few, included the giants of progressive Urdu and Hindi literature, Rajinder Singh Bedi, Krishan Chander, Ismat Chughtai, Ali Sardar Jafri, and Ahmad Nadeem Qasimi; editors of literary journals Baburao Patel and Diwan Singh Maftoon; journalist-poets like Agha Khalash Kashmiri; acclaimed artist M. A. Rahman Chughtai; icons of the Bombay film industry like actors Ashok Kumar and Shyam; producers S. Mukherjee and V. Shantaram; directors K. Asif and Shaukat Hussain Rizvi; lyricist Raja Mehdi Ali Khan; music directors Rafique Ghaznavi and Khurshid Anwar—not to mention the peerless nightingale of united India and Melody Queen of Pakistan, Madam Noor Jahan.

In his brutally candid sketches in *Bald Angels* on celebrities he came to know well, Manto made creative uses of his personal memory to give glimpses into the subcontinent's collective social and cultural history that have been obscured in the mayhem and dislocations of partition or swept aside by the torrent of selective nationalist reconstructions of the past. He was also a diligent archivist who preserved letters written to him by literary associates, as well as by admirers and critics. This correspondence was the one treasure he took the trouble of bringing with him to Lahore. Most of Manto's own letters are not available, but his sketches and essays fill some key gaps. The individuals and events he wrote about, with his powers of keen and candid observation, were temporally, if not spatially, immediate to him. As a result, his writings evince a more effective coincidence of personal memory and collective history than do narrations of the past relying on the retrieval of memories several decades down the line.

Manto's days are immortalized in his own and other people's writings. The rhythms of Bombay, its electric cars, breathtaking ocean views, exotic eateries, foul-smelling alleyways, and curious dialects struck intimate and enduring chords within him. Trying to make a living by working in the film industry, however, where art for art's sake had no value, was frustrating and demoralizing. After entering the glitzy and competitive world of Bombay cinema, Manto had no qualms about trying to find employment for struggling fellow writers like Rajinder Singh Bedi (1915–1984), Krishan Chander (1914–1977), and Ahmad Nadeem Qasimi (1916–2006), even before he had found his own feet. As partial compensation for his indulgence, Manto solicited their opinions regularly on his film scripts. In letter after letter he urged Qasimi to move to Bombay. Desperately poor, Manto had the generosity of heart to offer to pay Qasimi's rail fare from Lahore and put him up in Bombay. He admitted to being a rash spender but promised to ensure that there would be books to read even if there was no food to eat.[5] Manto's altruism is all the more remarkable as the two had never met.

On being urged to come to Bombay to try his luck in the film industry, Bedi was tempted. He had never seen the ocean. But he could not bring himself to leave his modest job as a clerk at the Lahore Post Office for the uncertain risks of India's most glamorous city. He was content to just communicate with Manto, whom he greatly admired and sought to emulate. "You were the first to set this ball of progressivism in our literature rolling," Bedi wrote, and "I am glad you have still your shoulders to the wheel."[6] "Your transgressions of the frontiers of ethics have been extremely enjoyable," and in the "shariat of literature they are extremely heartwarming."[7] Responding to Manto's criticism about his prose being unduly convoluted and dense, Bedi conceded that soon after he started writing, someone questioned his command over the Urdu language, and he responded by using more difficult Urdu. "Don't think I did not like your criticism," he assured Manto. "In fact I am prepared to go so far as to admit that no other friend of mine has helped me emerge as a writer more than Manto," Bedi confessed. "So identify my literary weaknesses and also advise me how to remove them."[8]

Even before they met for the first time in Delhi, Krishan Chander had been won over by Manto's literary talents. Chander had been electrified by Manto's sensitive portrayal of

a prostitute named Saugandhi in "Hatak," which he printed
in the literary journal he edited, *Naye Zaviyah*. In his opinion, not only was "Hatak" the best Urdu short story; it had
no parallel in international literature.[9] He had read Russian
and French literature extensively and also Mirza Hadi Ruswa's
classic Urdu novel *Umrao Jan Ada* (1905) on the subject of
prostitution. But Chander thought Manto's sympathetic
treatment of Saugandhi's character was unmatched in any of
these works. With a few strokes of the pen Manto had un-
covered every aspect of a prostitute's role in society. Despite
selling her body, Saugandhi retains the purity of her soul in-
tact. Perceptive readers are left feeling that if she had not been
in the flesh trade, Saugandhi could have been a *devadasi*—
literally, servant of god—at some temple. After "Hatak" was
critically acclaimed, Manto published more stories, and his
name spread among the reading population like a flash of
light.[10] Impressed by Manto's broad-minded views on society
and his overall technical superiority, Chander willingly placed
himself under his tutelage in cinematic matters.[11] "What can
I say to you?" he wrote, after reading Manto's film script *Steel*
about the dismal working conditions of industrial labor and
their resistance against exploitation. He liked the story line,
especially its biting sarcasm and humor, and thought each
scene was superbly conceived from a cinematographic point
of view. Yet he was pessimistic: what director would dare take
on a script in which Manto had given free expression to his
socialist-cum-revolutionary beliefs? How could they write
about things they believed in and convey them to the general
public when men of finance controlled the film world? In financial difficulties, as Manto was, Krishan Chander was des-
perate to gain entry into the Bombay film industry. He com-

plained of mental stress, depletion, extreme unhappiness, and a desire to quit his existing job to start afresh.[12]

Getting fired from *Musawwir* in 1940 proved fortuitous for Manto in one respect. Through pure coincidence he ended up joining All-India Radio's Urdu Service in New Delhi, where Krishan Chander had recently been employed as a drama producer. This has led to speculation about Chander's role in getting Manto the job at All-India Radio. In fact, Manto had applied for the semigovernmental position before his dismissal from *Musawwir*. The editor of *Humayun*, Hamid Ali Khan, wrote him a glowing letter of introduction.[13] After receiving the letter of appointment offering him a monthly salary of 150 rupees, Manto quickly packed a few things and traveled in a first-class compartment on the Frontier Mail from Bombay to Lahore. There, on 13 December 1940, Abu Saeed Qureshi and Hasan Abbas met him at the train station. Abbas and Bari were sharing a small room in Lahore's Old Anarkali Bazaar near the Nagina Bakery. This is where the three friends headed for a drunken night of animated conversation and smoke. They were joined by Bari and, later on, also by Rajinder Singh Bedi and the leftist activist Abdullah Malik. A memorable night in many ways, it lacked the intensity of the days Manto, Bari, Abu Saeed, and Abbas had spent discussing, researching, and writing in Dar-ul-Ahmar in Amritsar.[14]

Bidding farewell to his closest friends in Lahore, Manto embarked on a new chapter in his career, though he was no stranger to the world of radio. Radio stations in Bombay, Lahore, Lucknow, and New Delhi had been airing his plays and skits for the past few years. On his way to take up the position of staff artist at All-India Radio in New Delhi, Manto stopped in Amritsar. There, on 28 December 1940, sitting in the familiar space of Dar-ul-Ahmar, he wrote the preface for his first anthology of short humorous plays, entitled *Aao* (Come). In the collection—part of a critical tradition associated with the late nineteenth-century satirist Akbar Allahabadi—the names of all ten plays started with "Come"; by Manto's standards, they constituted a relatively temperate critique of the unthinking imitation of Western thought and practices. Manto wrote the plays over a period of about five months. The three main characters, Lajwanti, her husband, Kishore, and his brother Narayan, reappear in all the plays. All the plays begin with Lajwanti's invitation to Kishore—for instance, "Come Let's Write a Story"; "Come Let's Play Cards"; "Come Listen to the Radio"; "Come Let's Steal"; and "Come Let's Lie." With his characteristic sarcasm, Manto pokes fun at those who unthinkingly adopt Western culture, and raises a variety of social and political issues. In his usual candid style, he described the plays "as a product of the daily struggle to feed his stomach, a challenge that confronted every Urdu writer in India until he was completely paralyzed mentally." "I was hungry and so wrote these dramas," he divulged. "What I seek is appreciation for the few humorous dramas my mind has produced via my stomach, and which have made people laugh but not brought the faintest smile to my lips."[15]

On arriving in the imperial capital, Manto headed to Krishan Chander's residence in Delhi's Tees Hazari neighborhood. They finally met in person when, upon returning from his office, Krishan Chander saw a lanky and fair-complexioned stranger wearing a long coat and carrying a small leather bag. "You are Krishan Chander?" the visitor asked. "Manto?" was the reply. The two embraced each other. Manto lost no time making himself comfortable, thinking nothing of chastis-

12

Manto with Abu Saeed Qureshi
(seated on extreme right) and
friends, no date

ing Chander for his taste for cheap cigarettes and his cook's
strange bent for frying fresh chapatis in oil. Krishan Chander
claims never to have drunk alcohol in his life. However, he
did not have the heart to dampen Manto's enthusiasm when
he produced a bottle of Solan whiskey from the leather bag
and offered him a peg. They talked late into the night, with

Manto urging his friend to quit Delhi for the razzmatazz of Bombay. Chander fell asleep on the sofa. Manto dozed off on the chair, his neck pressed against his uplifted legs. In the morning, Manto asked for whiskey, saying it was the best way to eliminate the taste of alcohol, as he had to go to All-India Radio (AIR). When a surprised Krishan Chander asked why, Manto revealed that he had been appointed as a dramatist. "But last night you were sending me off to Bombay to work in films," Chander said, looking confused. "To hell with Bombay; stop this rubbish, send for some whiskey," Manto said. He then opened his bag, pulled out a short story, and gave it to Krishan Chander to read. "I don't show my stories to anyone," Manto said, "not even my father." "I am showing it to you, though you too don't write very well," he teased, "but there is one thing about your stories that I appreciate, understand, Krishan Chander, M.A?"[16]

It was the onset of one of the more creative and memorable phases of Manto's life. The AIR office was in a large bungalow on Alipur Road. Established in 1936, a mere fourteen years after the first play was aired on the BBC, AIR had been broadcasting radio dramas from its inception. Radio was a major attraction for educated youth looking for gainful employment during World War II. "Like the Qaf Mountains,[17] radio was full of fairies, music, dance, plays—Akhtari Bai Faizabadi, Anwar Bai Agrawalli, Veenapani Bahaduri, Deepali Talukdar—in short it was Raja Inder's assemblage (a fairyland)."[18] While this starry-eyed view from the outside needs to be qualified by the hard realities of working at AIR, there can be no denying the quality of the musical and literary talent that had congregated under one roof. Apart from Krishan Chander and the progressive Urdu poet N. M. Rashid, who was director of AIR's Urdu Service, Manto had the opportunity to work with and get to know several heavyweights of Urdu and Hindi literature, including Upendranath Ashk, Balwant Singh Gargi, Chiragh Hasan Hasrat, Raja Mehdi Ali Khan, Miraji, Akhtar Hussain Raipuri, Rafi Pir, and Devendra Satyarthi. Rajinder Singh Bedi joined for a while, as did Ahmad Nadeem Qasimi, who wrote an opera-length poem for the first time during this period.

Manto was the star by far. His extraordinary self-esteem irked fellow writers with inflated egos or a chip on their shoulder. Manto's inclination for mischief occasionally led to bad blood. Satyarthi and Bedi were incensed at Manto for writing the story "Taraqi Pasand" (Progressive). A hilarious yarn based on an actual incident involving Bedi and Satyarthi, it revolves around an aspiring young Sikh writer whose home is taken over by an older "Progressive" writer. Manto had heard Bedi speak of the time when Satyarthi was transitioning from writing folk songs to crafting short stories. While staying with Bedi in Lahore with his entire family, Satyarthi insisted on reading his freshly scripted stories out loud morning and evening, leaving the host no time to spend with his wife and children. After Manto's "Taraqi Pasand" created a stir in Delhi literary circles, Satyarthi retaliated with a story called "Naye Devta" (New Gods), which was overseen by Bedi. The Urdu poet Faiz Ahmad Faiz was also said to have had a hand in the story. In a dig at Manto's impeccably laundered clothes and personal cleanliness, the main character is called Nifasat (Neatness) Hasan. The story opens with a question. How can Nifasat Hasan, who is famous for his rebellious opposition to the exploitation of labor by capital's widening trap, take up a job in a semigovernmental establishment, like a fly caught in a web? To make matters worse, he was inviting friends to join him in his captivity. The witty take on Nifasat (read Saadat) Hasan's personality—his habits, anger, alcohol sprees, irritability, egoism, and appetite for topics bordering on the perverse, like sexuality—as well as hits on his other weaknesses, riled Manto.[19] Satyarthi later attributed the rancor to their having spent an excessive amount of time together and claimed to hold him in high esteem.[20]

Manto's run-ins with Upendranath Ashk (1910–1996) were more instinctive. He did not think well of Ashk and kept him at arm's length. The friction between them stemmed from literary and personal differences. Before they met in person, Ashk had openly criticized one of Manto's characters, Khushia, as unconvincing. Ashk had published a few well-known collections of short stories and fancied his credentials as an original writer. He had a sneaking contempt for Saadat Hasan, whom he first heard of as a translator of Russian literature from English to Urdu. "Naturally, while reading 'Khushia' I was already opposed to the writer," Ashk confessed. Indeed, he did not think much of "Khushia," though it is considered to be one of Manto's better stories. Ashk conceded that Manto dealt well with the plot, but given that Khushia is a pimp, his high-minded love for a young prostitute, Kanta, whom he has accidentally seen stark naked, lacked realism. Ashk had a friend who regularly visited the red-light district and could say with conviction that pimps routinely used a prostitute's body before putting her in the business. Khushia was a creation of Manto's mind, not a realistic character. When Bedi asked for Ashk's opinion of "Khushia," Ashk impetuously said it was "a two-paisa" or worthless story. During one of his tiffs with Manto in Delhi, Bedi conveyed Ashk's view of Khushia to Manto.[21]

One day Ashk was sitting in Krishan Chander's empty office when Manto, whose workplace was close by, came by casually and said: "I know that you did not like my story 'Khushia'; what did you not like about it?" Ashk maintains that he told Manto to cool off. He had been hired as a Hindi writer and was not in competition with him. People wanted them to fight so that they could enjoy the spectacle. "Why should we give them that pleasure?" When Manto persisted in asking what he did not like about "Khushia," Ashk remembers saying something to this effect: "You had an idea and you placed yourself in the role of the pimp and wrote the story. In real life if Khushia had really been a pimp and Kanta had appeared before him nude, he would have grabbed her instantly. What you wrote can be thought of by an educated poet; not an illiterate pimp." Manto kept quiet for a bit and then exasperatedly said: "Yes, yes, I am that pimp; Manto is that pimp. What do you know about storytelling? What do you write yourself?"

While he did not think much of Ashk as a poet, writer, and human being, Manto helped get him a job at the production company Filmistan. In his well-known essay "Manto Mera Dushman" (Manto My Enemy), Ashk denies any personal animosity between the two. On the second or third day after his arrival in Bombay, as they were sitting face-to-face in a victoria going down Grant Road, Manto turned to Ashk and said, "I like you though I hate you."[22] The cryptic remark sums up the relationship that has come to be remembered as a personality clash of withering proportions. Ashk rued being declared Manto's enemy before meeting him, and he resented being the stalking horse for others harboring personal grudges against a notoriously rebellious and daring writer. The snide dedication in the book version of "Manto Mera Dushman"

office space. Krishan Chander claimed that they wrote profusely, and with hope and freshness. Manto's pen was amaz-
ingly prolific, and every other day he composed a play, a feature, or a story. Krishan Chander thought that Manto wrote
his best stories and plays during this time, and later explored
the possibility of getting an anthology of the dramas published.[27] Commissioned to write radio dramas and features,
Manto began churning out material with lightning speed on
his Urdu and English typewriters, sitting in his trademark
crouching position, feet on the chair. In an acknowledgment
of his stellar work, Krishan Chander issued a formal circular
on behalf of the government of India's broadcasting corpora-
tion on 14 August 1941 in appreciation of Manto's contributions to AIR. He was "the first person" to write radio plays
on war topics in Hindustani, the name used for spoken Urdu,
that "have now become very popular with our listeners."[28]

Manto's lively personality and sharp repartee made him a
much sought-after figure at AIR. Radio artists heard him read
his plays aloud, drank tea at Manto's expense, and flatteringly
called him "the king of drama."[29] On the rare occasions that
he showed up for a drama rehearsal, Krishan Chander has
remembered, his verbal fireworks created such a pleasant atmosphere that the effect lasted for several hours afterwards.[30]
Giving a less positive spin to the overall scene at AIR, Ashk
claims that toadies and friends constantly surrounded his
bête noire, who was respectfully referred to as "Manto Sahib."
Ashk attributes the deference to "some relative of Manto's"
who was the secretary at the Ministry of Information and
Broadcasting.[31] Quite apart from the unlikelihood that an
Indian would have been an information ministry secretary in
the early 1940s, Manto had no relative senior enough in the

colonial bureaucracy to cover his back; Ashk's unfair charge showed him up as an enemy friend.

"The difference between life in Bombay and here is like heaven and earth," Manto wrote to Qasimi. "There I stayed well clear of enemy friends, but here one has to meet a lot of people who cause a lot of consternation."[32] A modernist who lived in the present, Manto took to his responsibilities at AIR with such aplomb that he attracted awe and respect even among those who disapproved of his drinking habits and barbed tongue. While older writers fell by the wayside, he successfully adapted his writing to the radio medium. His friend and biographer Abu Saeed Qureshi has aptly remarked that it was radio that made Saadat Hasan "Manto." Millions heard his radio plays and called him Manto; only his close friends and relatives knew him as Saadat. In the audio world, Abu Saeed thought Manto had the same status as Charlie Chaplin did in films. "Like Chaplin, Manto was an individualist whose imprint has been left for all times."[33] He authored more than a hundred plays and features during his brief stint at All-India Radio in Delhi. AIR's stations in key cities broadcast these, making him a household name. With World War II at its height, Manto was one of the first to write Urdu features and radio plays on the subject of war. Among the most famous of his radio plays was *Journalist*, a biting critique of newspaper proprietors and their exploitation of journalists. The play created an uproar in journalistic circles, forcing AIR's otherwise enlightened station director Patras Bukhari to prohibit the rebroadcast of *Journalist*. Manto's main character was his mentor-friend Bari Alig—a sympathetic portrayal of a man he had come to love and, despite all his faults, respect. Working tirelessly at a newspaper whose proprietor had not paid him a salary for four years, Bari reached the end of his tether when the local paanwallah (betel nut seller) refused to give him any more credit for cigarettes. Demanding his money, he told the miserly proprietor: "You serve the nation. I serve the nation, this newspaper and you, but I have never received remuneration for this on time or, one should say, at any time. In four months you have given me Rs.16. Fear God, I am a human being. I get hungry . . . sometimes I even feel like eating sweets. You made me this paper's editor, not a sanyasi [a Hindu religious mendicant] or a sadhu [ascetic] who has forsaken the world." With the everyday suffering of journalists as the peg, the play proceeds to discuss the issues of the day: the near and distant causes of the outbreak of war with Germany and the subsequent recruitment drive. A sober voice of knowledge and reason, Bari tries educating a few brawling drunkards in the local tavern about the gravity of the war in Europe and its as-yet-unknown consequences for the world.[34]

The world war also provided the backdrop for other plays, like *Eid Card*. But socially relevant issues constituted the core of Manto's dramatic themes. His radio play *Jaib Katra* (Pickpocket) is easily his most notable achievement from his days at AIR. It is a moving story about a good-hearted expert pickpocket, Kashi, who falls in love with a schoolteacher, Bimla, whose bag he had pilfered. To ensure perfect immunity from the crime, he chops off his fingers. The climax is reached when Bimla needs Kashi to steal a bundle of letters containing her most personal secret from the pocket of a foxy pandit who is trying to extort a huge sum of money for them. Manto's main point is that society or external factors produce criminals, who, despite transgressing the norms, are human like anyone else and therefore susceptible to the reforming powers of love.[35] Manto believed in the basic goodness of human nature and blamed society for pushing people into degrading themselves by becoming criminals and prostitutes.

All too conscious of his worth and supremely proud of his abilities, Manto exuded staggering confidence, claiming he could write on any theme under the sun. This was no ordinary boast, as radio plays had to be written within the constraints of the limited pool of available actors. His colleagues turned this into a source of amusement, betting a dozen bottles of beer on Manto's writing plays with odd names like *Kabutri* (literally, a female pigeon). Once, while Manto was pondering over an off-the-wall theme, someone came to the door and said, "May I come in?" Manto was immediately challenged to write a play by that name, which he did promptly. On another occasion, he was called upon to produce a feature or a play after a writer canceled a scheduled program at the last minute. Manto refused, saying that even a machine needed time. Everyone begged him, and when one friend rolled a sheet of paper into his typewriter, Manto sat down and wrote *Intizar* (Waiting), a psychodrama that is considered to be one of his finest radio plays.[36] Eighteen of Manto's radio plays were published in 1940, as *Manto kay Dramay*, by Lahore's Naya Idara press. In the volume's preface, Manto points out that the technique he used in the plays was different from that of ordinary radio dramas. He had resolved the problem posed by the change of scenes by creating a few conventions, well aware that these would rankle professional critics and conservative commentators. Until alternative ways could be developed to deal with the alternation of scenes, it was useless to carp and complain about what was being attempted. Since he was "ahead of everyone else in this field," Manto was convinced that professional and amateur critics would find useful things in his plays. He encouraged everyone to hear the plays on the radio, as that was the medium for which they were written. Listening to the plays, which he had altered for publication, would allow critics to better gauge his lapses as well as their own failings, because "that is how I identified my flaws."[37]

Things were going well for Manto at work, and, what was more, he was almost happy. At 150 rupees a month he could afford to live relatively comfortably in a two-room flat with a large verandah in Hasan Building, a three-storied structure on Nicholson Road behind Kashmiri Gate. For neighbors he had his school friend Hasan Abbas and, after February 1942, also Abu Saeed Qureshi.[38] Before moving into his own flat, Abu Saeed lived with Manto and Safia in their flat for nearly six months. He thought their domestic life was blissful and the balance between them exemplary. It was not as if the two did not fight. They did so often, but they respected each other. Despite his heavy drinking, Manto was never violent. He loved to help around the house, and preparing the salad was his specialty. Safia cleaned while Manto did the ironing. There were always two or three kinds of dishes on the table. Always in a hurry, Manto seemed to be swallowing his food without chewing. Since he could not entirely sustain his life-style on what he earned at All-India Radio, Manto wrote for magazines like *Saqi* and published collections of his stories, radio features, and dramas, in addition to penning film scripts like *Banjara* for Seth Jagat Narain with Krishan Chander's help. Ahmad Nadeem Qasimi was summoned to write the lyrics for the film. In the early summer of 1942, Lahore's Maktaba-i-Urdu brought out his play series *Teen Auratain*, for which Manto's one-line preface was "Women themselves are the preface of Adam's story."[39] Among Delhi's publish-

of his elder brother and break its nose. On other occasions, Saeed imagined his friend making an idol of his mother and clutching it tightly to his chest. Like rain and sunshine at the same time, Manto's laughter was infused with bitter tears that no one could quite detect. He hated being pitied, preferring to bear his pain quietly and stoically.[42]

Manto conveyed the intense emotional upheaval caused by his son's death in a short story called "Khalid Mian."[43] His mental agony was aggravated by the need to defend himself against charges of obscenity for his story "Kali Shalwar," published by the annual Lahore journal *Adab-i-Latif* in 1942. It was the first of several cases brought against him under section 292 of the Indian Penal Code. The case was dismissed, but the charge of obscenity remained a severe provocation for Manto. "I am not a pornographer but a story writer," he was to defend himself over and over again for the rest of his life.[44] Ahmad Nadeem Qasimi thought the government of India ought to have booked Manto for "Naya Qanun," which had clear political overtones. If they had, Manto would have defied the colonial government by writing more politically inspired short stories. By charging him with obscenity for "Kali Shalwar," the colonial authorities had irritated him into writing a succession of stories dealing with prostitution and sexuality, like "Bu" (Odor) and "Dhuan" (Smoke) before partition and the classic "Thanda Gosht" (Colder than Ice) afterwards.[45]

"Delhi is a very bad place," Manto complained in July 1942. "I swear on God it has enforced stagnation on me."[46] He was reacting to the changed dynamics at the All-India Radio office after the well-known Urdu poet N. M. Rashid, successfully plotted to get Krishan Chander posted to Lucknow. With his main supporter out of the way, Manto became an easier target for those miffed by his overconfidence. Ashk, for one, saw an opportunity to avenge Manto's condescending attitude toward him. AIR was broadcasting three of Manto's plays each month, providing a meddlesome producer with scope to make whimsical interventions. So Ashk intrigued with Chander's replacement to have parts of Manto's play *Awara* (Vagabond) revised. Manto hit the roof. He would not let anyone alter a single word of what he wrote. Instead of caving in to bureaucratic dictation, Manto stormed out of All-India Radio clasping his Urdu typewriter, never to return again.[47]

Prior to this incident, Manto had felt that his achievements in radio, in terms of both innovation and popularity with listeners, justified him a place on the front page of publications like *Awaz* (Sound) and *Indian Listener*. But when he crossed the one hundred mark with his plays and features, much like a cricketer proud of reaching a century, all Manto got were a few lines of mention in these radio journals. Tired of writing for radio with such mixed rewards, he started corresponding with film companies in Bombay. In July 1942 he heard that Hind Pictures was producing one of his screenplays, *Hartal* (Strike).[48] "Let's go, Safia," he would say. "So let's go, as if I have anyone here," Safia replied, delighted at the prospect of returning to Bombay where her mother and two younger sisters lived.[49] The matter was decided when Manto's old friend Nazir Ahmad Ludhianvi offered him the editorship of *Musawwir* once again, with the added incentive of the possible opportunity to write a screenplay for Shaukat Hussain Rizvi, a director whose last film had made a killing at the box office. With so many positive memories of Bombay fresh in his mind, and good chances of finding gainful employment in the film industry, it was an offer Manto could not refuse.

Muslim states" aimed at winning Muslims an equitable share of power in independent India, based on their religious majorities in the northwestern provinces of Punjab, NWFP (the North-West Frontier Province), Sindh, and Baluchistan, and Bengal and Assam in the northeast.[51] Widely interpreted in India as a "separatist" demand, the Muslim League's policy of cooperation with the colonial government and insistence on "Pakistan" intensified Hindu-Muslim tensions. Relations between the two communities became especially strained after the Muslim League asked its supporters to stay away from the Quit India movement.

Detached but not indifferent to the politics of the Congress and the Muslim League, Manto observed their fallout on everyday social relations. In 1942 he wrote an essay, "Hindustan ko Lidroon say Bachao" (Save India from Leaders), placing the blame for the stresses and strains in relations between India's two main communities on the insincerity of political leaders. After giving heated speeches slamming capitalism at public meetings, they went home to sleep in their comfortable beds. Not even a fraction of their nights was spent figuring out what ailed India collectively, as they were too busy diagnosing their own particular diseases. It was distasteful to hear politicians, who could not keep their own homes in order, talking about rectifying the affairs of the homeland and giving people lessons in ethics. Politicians talked incessantly of religion, claiming it was in danger when they had never followed its basic tenets. "Religion is what it was and will always stay that way," Manto wrote; "the spirit of religion is a concrete reality that will never change." "Religion is like a rock unaffected by the waves of the sea" and could not be in danger. If a danger existed, it was from leaders who endangered religion for their own personal ends. These so-called leaders, who "carried the corpse of politics and religion on their shoulders" and told gullible people they could make the dead come alive again, were interested only in lining their own pockets with goods stolen from the poor. India's young men, with their torn shirts, needed to overthrow such a leadership from the heights they had wrongly come to occupy. Poverty was not a curse. The poor man rowing his own boat was far better off than the rich. India's deprived and dispossessed millions needed to determine their own best interests and just sit back and watch the spectacle of would-be leaders trying to navigate their weighty ships on the vast ocean of life.[52]

Manto's negative view of politicians who peddle religion for self-glorification drew on a philosophy of life that firmly rejected deception and hypocrisy. Compared to the shop-keepers of religion, whose hearts are dark and filled with hatred, his prostitutes, pimps, and criminals are truer to their humanity. He had seen through the politically motivated nature of the Hindu-Muslim problem as early as 1936 and was prompted to compose an appeal for the residents of Bombay.[53] His passion for Bombay and warm memories of the days he spent there were based on the city's unique ability to bring talented people from various class and regional backgrounds together without the imposition of the religious and ideological barriers that were being invoked in the political discourse. From Manto's perspective, the preoccupations of the Congress and the Muslim League were at a considerable remove from the hard realities of everyday life about which he wrote stories, most notably "Nara" (Slogan).

One evening after coming back to Bombay, Manto was as usual squatting on a large chair in *Musawwir*'s office on Clare

Road, alternately contemplating the quickening of the political pace on the streets outside and toying with ideas for a film script that could fetch good money, when he had an encounter that was to leave a lasting impression on him. Shahid Latif, an acquaintance from Manto's Aligarh days and also a writer, walked in with his wife, Ismat Chughtai. Her scandalous short story "Lihaf" (Quilt), about sexual relations between women, had been published a month earlier in Ahmad Nadeem Qasimi's *Adab-i-Latif.* Manto had read the story while he was still at All-India Radio. He liked it but told Krishan Chander that Qasimi should have deleted its last sentence, since it showed a lack of craft. The objectionable final line read: "Even if someone gives me a lakh of rupees, I won't tell anyone what I saw when the quilt was lifted by an inch." The ever-observant Manto recalled meeting an unassuming woman. Her sharp eyes sparkling behind thick-rimmed glasses and cheeks dimpling at the barest of smiles, Ismat was dressed in a simple white sari with a small border and a tight-fitting black-and-white striped blouse; she wore flat brown sandals and carried a small handbag. "I liked your story," he said, "but why did you ruin it with the utterly pointless last line?" "What's wrong with that sentence?" Ismat asked, a little taken aback. He kept quiet after seeing the embarrassed look on her face, an expression much like that of any ordinary young woman who had heard something unutterable.[54] The ultimate shock for him came when Ismat said she regretted writing "Lihaf," as it had caused her endless trouble, and did not think it was a literary classic.[55] As she got up to leave, a disappointed Manto told himself, "The wretch, she turned out to be a woman after all!"[56]

"Manto was a very sweet man, not at all vulgar-minded," Ismat reminisced several years later. "He was very sweet-looking, innocent, like a saint," she contended. Whenever she said that, Manto retorted: "I'm not a saint; I'm a very bad man."[57] Much to the chagrin of a contingent of their admirers, the two did not fall in love. "Instead, my wife fell for her," Manto recorded, impishly adding that if Safia had expressed her love, Ismat would almost certainly have chided her and said: "What cheek! Men of your father's age have fallen for me!"[58] The two women struck up a special friendship that outlasted the test of partition and Manto's premature death. On the day of their initial meeting, Ismat had struggled to overcome her nervousness about meeting the renowned short story writer. The initial formalities soon gave way to a surreal familiarity; she felt as if they had known each other since childhood. They argued, agreed and disagreed strongly, liked each other intensely, and became friends for life. If they planned to meet for five minutes, it ended up being a five-hour exchange.[59] Manto took to calling Ismat "Sister," and she reciprocated by referring to him as "Brother."

Circumstances brought them closer together than they might have wanted after they were both arrested under the same colonial obscenity law. At the time Manto was facing charges under section 30 of the Defense of India Act, for saying false and derogatory things about the colonial state's military forces in an essay he had read at Bombay's Jogeshwari College in January 1944.[60] The piece was later published in *Adab-i-Latif*'s annual number alongside his short story "Bu" (Odor), for which Manto was booked on grounds of obscenity. Nothing in Manto's brilliant essay on modern literature justifies the colonial objection. But he had evidently offended colonial sensibilities by writing a story about a young man, Randhir, who likes sleeping with Anglo-Indian women. Following the outbreak of the war, most of them join the specially created auxiliary force or end up servicing British soldiers. So Randhir turns to satisfying his lust with a low-caste woman. Many years later, still haunted by the sexual encounter, he spends his wedding night remembering the woman's body odor.

While the case against "Bu" was sub judice, Saqi Book Depot in Delhi brought out a second edition of Manto's book *Dhuan*, which contained the stories "Dhuan" and "Kali Shalwar," for both of which he had been tried and acquitted.[61] He was charged with obscenity yet again. As in the past, the attention of the colonial government was drawn by the press, in this case an irate article in the Lahore *Tribune* on 25 May 1944 entitled "Traffic in Obscene Literature." The article also mentioned Ismat Chughtai's recently published book *Chotain* (Injuries) as an example of obscene writings. It was Ismat's first brush with the law. Fortunately for the two friends, their arrests were illegal, as no warrant had been issued. But they had to make personal appearances in the Lahore District Courts until their acquittal on 1 June 1946. On their first visit, Manto and Ismat, accompanied by their spouses, made the best of a bad situation and had a wonderful time in Lahore, where they were feted and hailed as celebrities both within and outside the court. Manto met up with his old school buddies, Hasan Abbas and Abu Saeed Qureshi, both of whom were based in Lahore. However, the crowning moment of Manto's and Ismat's two trips to the city was a not-to-be-missed visit to a shoe shop specializing in handcrafted Mughal footwear, where they each bought about a dozen pairs on each occasion.[62] Even the fiercely independent-minded Ismat could not resist emulating Manto's highly developed obsession with shoes.

Manto and Ismat were drawn to each other even more because of the vigorous cosmopolitan cultural and intellectual milieu of Bombay in which they struggled to succeed as writers, while lending it their own distinctive coloring. Spring is the time for cavorting with abandon during Holi—the Hindu festival of colors, during which many people belonging to different faiths sprinkle colored powder and water on one another in joyous celebration of the coming of spring. Manto's film script *Chal Chal Re Naujawan* (Carry on Young Man), starring Ashok Kumar and Naseem Bano, was being shot at Filmistan. On the day of Holi, Manto was drinking with Shahid Latif on the balcony of his and Ismat's flat in Malad when they heard a commotion outside. A group of Filmistan employees, carrying coloring gear and dead set on partying, was at the gate. S. Mukherjee, the producer of *Chal Chal Re Naujawan*, was in the lead, with his cheerful and pudgy wife—Ashok Kumar's sister—marshaling the womenfolk. After protesting the intrusion momentarily, Ismat changed her mind and, along with Safia, joined the festivities. They started marching toward Naseem Bano's house, spraying all and sundry on Ghodbandar Road with blue, yellow, red, green, and black powders and dyes. Looking a sight, with her face and eyeglasses stained with psychedelic colors, Ismat was now the ringleader, her voice booming with a military commander's confidence as she smeared an oversized Bengali woman passing by with a thick layer of coal tar. Upon arriving at the famous film star's house, they found her in full makeup in a lovely light-colored sari. Somebody suggested she go and change. No sooner had Naseem Bano uttered the words "This is fine" than she was assaulted by the colors of Holi. The fairy-faced beauty queen of Bombay was transformed into a frightening multicolored witch, with gleaming white teeth and big eyes, evoking a painting by Behzad or Monet on which a child had splashed ink. Bored with throwing color on already grotesquely colored faces, the party turned to playing *kabadi*, a contact sport akin to wrestling. The men went first, followed by the women's more interesting match. There were peals of laughter each time the plump Mrs. Mukherjee fell to the ground. With her glasses coated in color, Safia invariably ended up running in the wrong direction, while Naseem remained stationary in a contrived attempt to show that she was unaccustomed to physical activity.[63]

Manto's account of the enchanting revelries in Bombay on Holi, bridging distinctions among different people through a haze of colorful merriment, is the more memorable when contrasted with the tortured memories of bloodletting that saturated the city's streets just a few years later. A contrarian by choice, who looked at most issues in novel ways, he found the mounting Hindu-Muslim tensions in his adopted home troubling and inexplicable. "I have never had any interest in politics and consider politicians and pharmacists to be one and the same." Elaborating the point, Manto mused:

Leadership and pharmacology are two professions whose practitioners use other people's prescriptions. What I mean to say is that I have as much interest in politics as Gandhiji has in cinema. Gandhiji does not see cinema, and I do not read newspapers. Actually, both of us are wrong. Gandhiji should see films and I ought to read newspapers.[64]

In the event, Manto took to reading newspapers, but neither Gandhi nor any of the other politicians made a beeline for the cinema hall. The successive failures of his films at the box office did not worry Manto so much as the deteriorating communitarian relations. "The Muslim League is a mosque; the Congress is a temple," he discovered; "this is what people think and that is what the newspapers say as well." The Congress wanted *swaraj* (independence) and so did the Muslim League. "But both have separate ways and do not work together because temple and mosque have nothing in common." He had reckoned that with all the disturbances taking place, Hindus and Muslims would come together through the mixing of their blood in the city's sewage. He was surprised to be proven completely wrong. From where he lived in Byculla, a long road snaked toward Mahim at the end of which there is a famous Muslim shrine. When the troubles reached this part of the city, boys pulled trees from the footpaths and started setting up roadblocks in the bazaar. When some Hindu boys began dragging a steel fence in the direction of the shrine, a few Muslims came forward and one of them said softly, "Look, don't go there . . . from here Pakistan starts," and sketched a line on the road. So the Hindu boys took the fence in the other direction, after which "no infidel made his way toward Pakistan."[65]

Manto's final years in undivided India had none of the allure often ascribed to them retrospectively. The dropping of the atom bomb on Hiroshima and Nagasaki saddened him immensely. Everything seemed futile. It was as if the present and the future had become meaningless.[66] He still loved Bombay but was far from happy with his circumstances. Defending himself against two obscenity cases was draining, emotionally and financially. His health suffered. He was diagnosed with water in his right lung. Safia's companionship and the birth of their daughter Nighat in July 1946 brought much-needed

13
Manto acting in
Eight Days (1946)

joy. Another important source of comfort during these trying times was friendship—most famously Manto's friendships with two of Bombay's top film heroes, Ashok Kumar
and Shyam. In *Bald Angels*, Manto talks about his close relations with Ashok Kumar, whom he referred to affection-
ately as "Dadamoni," which means elder brother in Bengali.
Ashok was a firm believer in the accuracy of astrology. While
they were still getting to know each other, he startled Manto
by saying that those with his horoscope had a son as a first

14

Poster of *Eight Days* (1946) with Ashok
Kumar. S.M.M. Ausaja collection

15

Credits for *Eight Days*. S.M.M. Ausaja
collection

child, a son who did not survive. Ashok had a similar astral configuration and revealed that his child was also a son and had been stillborn. As their relationship grew more intimate, their wives became good friends and shopped together often: a boon for Safia, as all the Bombay shopkeepers knew Ashok's wife and went out of their way to oblige them. Manto worked with Ashok on several films at Filmistan, most notably *Aath Din* (Eight Days), for which he wrote the script and made his acting debut as a shell-shocked soldier. The film was a commercial success and won him critical acclaim.

Meanwhile Manto's frustrations at Filmistan continued to mount. He felt slighted and let down by half-educated producers and directors, who made nonsense of his film scripts and forced him to write dialogues that he felt were beneath his dignity. When a filmmaker in Lahore offered him a job as consultant for 1,000 rupees a month, he seriously considered accepting.[67] He eventually recoiled at the prospect of leaving the Bombay film industry for the much smaller market in Lahore. Ashok Kumar, who had already quit Filmistan for Bombay Talkies, persuaded him to join him there. On 15 August 1947, the day India won freedom, Manto started work at Bombay Talkies, located on Churchgate Street, after signing a one-year contract. His job was to write dialogues and scenarios for all the films produced by the company, in addition to writing two original screenplays. For his labors Manto was given 850 rupees per month and promised an additional 5,000 rupees for the two film stories.[68] It was a far better deal than the one on offer in Lahore.[69] There was the added advantage of being in an environment where he could lock horns with a talented pool of people that included writers Kamal Amrohi, Ismat Chughtai, and Shahid Latif; lyricists Hasrat

16
Manto with Safia, Zakia (Safia's sister), and
Nighat, by Brij Mohan. Bombay, 1947

Lucknawi and Nazim Panipati; and music director Ghulam
Haider.[70]

India had been partitioned by the time Manto started working at Bombay Talkies. Punjab and other parts of North India
were in the grips of murderous violence. His wife and daughter

had left for Lahore, not so much to escape the violence as to enable Safia to prepare for the wedding of her youngest sister to Manto's favorite nephew and English translator, Hamid Jalal. They had the first taste of what was in the offing when, in early 1947, Manto's and his relatives' homes were burned and looted in Amritsar's Lawyers' Colony where he had grown up and first dreamed of revolution. The situation was tense in Delhi, where there had been random stabbings whose victims included tonga drivers working in noncurfew areas. Bombay too was unsettled. The presence of so many Muslims at Bombay Talkies provoked a strong reaction from the Hindu employees of the company, who began writing threatening letters anonymously to Ashok Kumar and his partner Savak Vacha. Manto recalled feeling guilty and raising the matter with Ashok, who retorted that it was a temporary madness, which would soon pass. To Manto's dismay, the madness seemed to be turning chronic, as the city descended into an orgy of violence.

One day, after spending time with Manto after work, Ashok was driving him home in his car when they passed through a rough Muslim neighborhood where no Hindu could dare go. A wedding party was coming toward them, and the moment Manto heard the sound of the accompanying band he grabbed Ashok's hand and said, "Dadamoni, where have you come?" "Not to worry," was the unnervingly calm response. Manto feared that Ashok would be immediately recognized; the murder of a famous Hindu would be quite an achievement for the thugs populating the area. Unable to remember a single Quranic verse and with his heart beating fast, Manto prayed: "O God, have mercy . . . please do not let a Muslim kill Ashok so that I have to carry the weight of his blood on my neck for the rest of my life. This is not the nation's neck, but mine, and yet it does not want to be lowered before another community for such an abominable act." As the car approached the wedding procession, people started shouting, "Ashok Kumar, Ashok Kumar." Manto froze, but Ashok kept his hands on the wheel in silence. Just as Manto was about to blurt out that he was a Muslim and Ashok was merely driving him home, two young men stepped forward and said calmly, "Ashok Bhai [brother], you won't find a way ahead, go via the adjoining side lane." If Ashok was their brother, Manto wondered, who am I? He looked at his *khadi* clothes—the mark of a Congress sympathizer—and wondered what they had made of him. Then perhaps they had not even noticed him in the presence of their matinee idol. As the car left the Muslim neighborhood, Manto heaved a sigh of relief. Ashok laughed and said: "You panicked for no reason; these people don't bother artists."[71]

The much-maligned mob had more capacity for discernment than he realized. For someone who abhorred the tyranny of the mob, it was a vignette that profoundly influenced Manto's understanding of partition violence. His graphically honest depictions of the bloodstained Holi played out on the subcontinental stage in the name of freedom were to condemn him in the courts of nationalism, whether Indian or Muslim, without the benefit of a fair trial. Manto had long ago anticipated the role he would have to play to constantly remind people of the porous frontiers between madness and civilization. In one of his earliest stories, "Inqilab Pasand" (Revolutionary), written on 24 March 1935, the main character responded to accusations of insanity by asserting:

> Think of me as a lawyer, who fights a legal battle that has already been lost . . . I am a repressed voice . . . humanity

is a face and I am a scream. . . . I am a deep-sea diver whom nature has drowned in the dusky depths of the sea . . . so that I can find something . . . I have brought back a precious pearl . . . of truth. . . . so that I can reveal the hidden side of life. . . . Humanity is a heart, and every person has the same kind of heart. If you want to cool the fires of your animal passions by violating the honor of a neighbor's girl . . . If your heart is dark and burned out, it is not your fault. The makeup of society is such that every roof is suppressing a neighbor's roof, every brick another brick.[72]

Throughout the remaining twelve years before the partition of India, Manto metaphorically donned the lawyer's garb and let out a volley of screams, damning the colonial rulers for their callous and unwarranted governance as well as demolishing the certitudes of nationalist pride, religious and secular.[73] Recollecting the bedlam caused by Hindu-Muslim violence during his last days in Bombay, he wrote that whenever he and his friends stepped out of the house, they made sure to take two caps with them, a Hindu cap and a Rumi cap. When they were passing a Muslim neighborhood, they wore the Rumi cap; when they entered a Hindu neighborhood, they put on the Hindu cap. "During this fracas we bought a Gandhi cap that we kept in our pockets and put on quickly whenever the need arose." Using the trope of changing caps for the assertion of religious identities in times of violence, Manto quipped, "Previously religion used to be in one's heart, now it's in caps. . . . Politics too operates through these caps. Long live caps!"[74]

Switching caps did not mean changing heart. In his most sensitive and moving sketch, "Murli ki Dhun"—literally, the sound of Krishna's flute—in the collection *Bald Angels*, Manto writes with affection about his very dear friend, the actor Shyam, who died tragically in April 1951 after falling off a horse during a film shoot. Shyam, whose real name was Sunder Shyam Chadha, came from Sialkot. He was a ladies' man and had innumerable affairs. The love of his life, however, was a Muslim woman, Mumtaz, better known as Taji, whom he married. They had two children, and their daughter, Sahira Kazimi, went on to make her mark as a highly successful actress and producer in the early decades of Pakistan Television. A lively and endearing personality, Shyam reminded Manto

17
Shyam and Taji.
Courtesy Sahira
Kazimi

of a character in a Russian novel. They both were heavy drinkers and bonded instantly. One of the standing jokes between them was the word "Heptulla," an unusual name Manto came across in the sports section of a newspaper, and which became an expression for anything out of the ordinary. A few months before partition, Shyam and Taji came to live with Manto in his new flat at 18 Oxford Chambers on Clare Road, where he had moved just before his wife and daughter left Bombay. After Taji left, following a major tiff with Shyam, the two had free rein to lead a "Heptulla" sort of existence. Despite being strapped for funds, they did not stint themselves in their drinking, which actually increased owing to the boredom of long curfew hours. Neither of them ever discussed money or who was spending more. When Shyam signed a film contract with Bombay Talkies and managed to get a few hundred rupees as an advance, he promptly shared it with Manto, who was completely broke at the time.[75]

The sharing and caring between the two friends was not disrupted by the violence that erupted with partition. Newspapers were filled with reports of ghastly massacres, rapes, and abductions, some of which were taking place just a few paces away from them. Their relationship remained unaffected except for one fleeting, but weighty, moment. Once they were listening to a family of Sikh refugees telling horrific stories about the killings perpetrated by Muslims in Rawalpindi. Manto could see that Shyam was extremely perturbed, and he understood the emotional turmoil his friend was undergoing. When they left the place, Manto said to him: "I am a Muslim, don't you feel like killing me?" Shyam replied in all seriousness: "Not now, but when I was hearing about the atrocities committed by Muslims . . . I could have killed you." Manto recalled being shocked by Shyam's words and confessed that he too might have killed his best friend under those circumstances. But when he thought about it afterwards, and there was a vast difference between then and now, he suddenly realized what lay at the roots of the bloodletting between Hindus and Muslims. Manto kept pondering over Shyam's words—not now, but at the time yes—and the answer, the pity of partition, hit him, the answer that lay in human nature itself.[76] The truth of what Shyam had said was the pearl Manto had been seeking in the newspapers every day. It left such a lasting impression on him that he reproduced his exchange with Shyam in the short story "Sahai," if only to prove that his fiction was nothing if it did not approximate the factual.

As 1947 drew to a close, Manto was finding it excruciatingly difficult to stay on in Bombay. His cosmopolitan vision could not come to terms with an atmosphere poisoned by an unabated cycle of killings, arson, and rape. The independence of Pakistan and India had been celebrated with great enthusiasm in Bombay, and the streets were reverberating with slogans and the names of Jawaharlal Nehru and Quaid-i-Azam Mohammad Ali Jinnah. Manto was confused. He could not decide whether India or Pakistan was his homeland. "Whose blood was being shed with such heartlessness every day? Where would they burn or bury the bones from which the vultures had stripped off the flesh of religion?" He could not help wondering whether, now that they were free, the people of the subcontinent ceased to be subjugated. And what would they dream of now that they were free from colonial servitude? Would they have their own slaves now? To each of these big questions, there was an Indian answer, a Pakistani answer, and a British answer. Some traced the answers to the

1857 rebellion, others to the East India Company's rule, while still others went further back and wanted to assess the role of the Mughal empire. "Everybody wanted to push further and further into the past, while the murderers and terrorists were moving ahead undeterred and writing a story of blood and fire to which there was no parallel in world history."[77]

To make matters worse, friction between Hindu and Muslim employees at Bombay Talkies had already unhinged Manto's mind when, quite unexpectedly, he experienced the disappointment of being marginalized and overlooked, something he simply could not abide. Ashok and Vacha turned down the screenplay he had written as part of his contractual obligations and preferred to film Kamal Amrohi's story "Mahal." Adding insult to what was already unbearable injury to Manto's pride and sensibility, his story failed to make even the second grade of films, and Ismat Chughtai's "Ziddi" was chosen instead. Matters came to a head when Manto's criticism of Nazir Ajmeri's story "Majboor" was dismissed with the allegation that he was biased because he himself was a story writer.[78] Feeling aggrieved, he stopped going to work. He drank excessively, but that brought no relief as he wasted the day lying on the sofa in his flat. Shyam tried leavening the atmosphere by cracking jokes, infuriating Manto even more.[79] Thinking back to the time Ashok Kumar was stopped in the Muslim neighborhood and told that there was no road ahead, he told himself, "Manto Bhai, this street will lead you nowhere; it's best to go via the adjoining side lane." And so he decided to take the side lane to Pakistan.[80]

After he had made up his mind to leave for Lahore, Manto started packing. He ran various errands, among them his visit to the washermen's colony, to collect his laundry, about which he wrote tellingly in the story "Ram Khalawan." When Shyam returned from an all-night shoot, he peered at the packed baggage and nonchalantly remarked, "Going?" Manto answered in the affirmative. Nothing further was said about the matter. When the time came for him to leave, Shyam poured two large pegs of brandy and said, "Heptulla." "Heptulla," Manto shot back. Shyam then threw his arms around him and said, "Swine." Holding back his tears, Manto replied, "Pakistani swine." Shyam shouted back in earnest, "Zindabad [Long live] Pakistan." "Zindabad Bharat [India]," Manto retorted before leaving for the port to board the ship taking him to Karachi. Shyam came with him all the way to the ship's deck, telling funny stories, as was his wont. When the gong sounded announcing the ship's departure, he said, "Heptulla" out loud, stepped down the gangway, and walked away without once looking back.[81]

Manto left Bombay without bidding farewell to several close friends, including Shahid Latif and Ismat Chughtai. Ismat was livid with him for absconding. At one level her grievance came from a genuine sense of loss at the sudden departure of two very close friends, Manto's so soon after Safia's. But at another level, the long shadow of partition politics was making itself felt. The creation of Pakistan divided the Muslims of the subcontinent into two hostile states. Those left behind in India resented what many considered as abandonment by their numerically predominant coreligionists in Pakistan. Ismat later wrote that Manto had asked her and Shahid to come with him, alleging that he spoke of the wonderful future awaiting them in Pakistan, where they would be allotted the abandoned bungalows of fleeing non-Muslims. "It will only be us there and we will advance very rapidly," Manto is supposed to have said. Disgusted by him, Ismat maintains that she started really hating him. Manto had turned out to be a coward; he had escaped to Pakistan to save his skin and, what was worse, now wanted to improve his own life by grabbing other people's property. Ismat mentions receiving ecstatic letters from him, inviting her and Shahid to Pakistan and promising to help get a cinema allotted in their name.[82] Manto may well have been pulling her leg; he may have said things in a drunken stupor. What is undeniable is that Ismat's claims fly in the face of all the available evidence. Manto did not make a killing at other people's expense. Though entitled to a reasonable-sized house in compensation for his ancestral home in Amritsar, he got nothing and lived in a modest flat that was allotted to his nephew, who transferred it into Manto's name. Life in Pakistan was anything but idyllic, as Ismat Chughtai must have known, given that she was in touch with both Manto and Safia. What is more, Manto wrote disparagingly of the clamor for allotments in newly independent Pakistan. The only one ever offered to him, paradoxically enough, was an ice factory, in 1954. It is unclear whether this was meant to be a joke or was an inadvertent "just reward" from a state whose welcoming gift to Manto was to charge him under the colonial obscenity laws for "Thanda Gosht"— literally, cold flesh, but translated as "Colder than Ice"[83]—his first short story on Pakistani soil.

"After leaving, Bombay I was sad," Manto wrote on 28 October 1951. He had loved the city and still did, because it was here that he had spent twelve years of his life, including his most difficult, happiest, and most memorable times. Bombay was "where I forged lasting friendships that I take pride in; I got married there; my first child was born there, and it is where my second child spent the first day of her life." At times in Bombay he survived on a few rupees, but there he also earned vast sums of money and lived in style. "The tumult wrought by the partition of the country made a rebel out of me for a long time, and I remain one," Manto disclosed. He claimed he had come to accept the "frightening reality" and did not let despair come anywhere near him.[84] Resignation did not mean forgiving, far less forgetting, the rivers of blood that had appeared to drown all sense of humanity in large swaths of the subcontinent. Disillusioned with the lack of opportunities available for him in his newly adopted country, and feeling unappreciated, Manto began drowning his sorrows in an excess of drink, an excess that turned the heavy drinker in him into an alcoholic in a land that was meant to be pure of such abominations.

The more Manto drank, the more he fell into debt. The more he fell into debt, the more money he borrowed from all and sundry, so much so that newspaper editors kept him within their sight until he completed a piece before making a payment. No one in the publishing business had any doubts about Manto's phenomenal talents, nor, for that matter, did anyone in Lahore's minuscule and cash-starved film industry, which was given a new lease on life by Shaukat Hussain Rizvi, Noor Jahan, and Khurshid Anwar. But appreciation without opportunity and adequate remuneration was cold comfort, particularly once he had been dealt a double blow—the Pakistani state charged him with obscenity, while his so-called progressive literary friends and admirers blacklisted him for being a reactionary. Hitting the bottle with a vengeance, he started keeping company with alcoholic "enemy friends," who knew nothing about literature and merely facilitated his goal of "committing physical and spiritual suicide" in the shortest possible time.[85]

Friends from across the border never ceased urging Manto to return to Bombay. Ashok Kumar wrote to him in broken Urdu asking him to come back, a letter to which Manto regretted never having responded.[86] Agha Khalash Kashmiri, a close friend from Manto's childhood days in Amritsar who still worked for *Musawwir*, wrote regularly from Bombay. Well aware of his friend's dire financial situation and failing health, Kashmiri expended time and energy tracking down film producers in India who owed money to Manto. The imposition of the border was never more intrusive than in the difficulties it created for writers and artists in the two countries who were due royalty and other payments. Kashmiri tried skirting the problem by urging Bombay filmmakers to ask their contacts in Karachi to send money to Manto. He pressed Manto to give up drinking and found it hard to imagine what Safia must be going through. "We talk about you often," Kashmiri wrote, referring to Nazir Ludhianvi, who was suffering from stomach cancer. Both Kashmiri and Ludhianvi thought Manto should visit Bombay to see what opportunities were available for him.[87] They were not the only ones.

"Everyone here misses you and feels the lack of your lively humor that you squandered on them so generously," Shyam wrote to him on 19 January 1948. Vacha found it ironic that Manto, who had objected to the hiring of Muslims at Bombay Talkies, had "run off to Pakistan" and "become a martyr of his own credo." Shyam did not necessarily agree with Vacha's viewpoint but thought decency demanded that Manto write to him.[88] It is unclear whether Manto wrote to Vacha. But he did make it a point to record not just Shyam's decency but

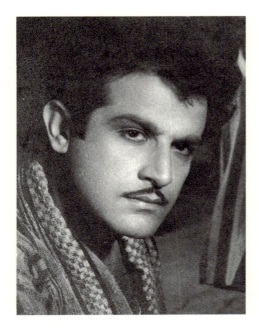

18
Shyam. Courtesy
Sahira Kazimi

also his generosity and solicitude as a friend despite the great divide of partition. As Manto's financial woes mounted, he received a letter at someone else's address saying that the owners of Tehseen Pictures wanted to meet him. He met with the owners and learned that they had been receiving a barrage of telegrams from Shyam in Bombay urging them to find Manto and give him five hundred rupees. Manto took the money, his eyes wet with emotion.[89]

The two friends had a rapturous reunion when Shyam visited Lahore briefly after partition for the release of his film. It was the same Shyam, full of smiles and laughter, but now he was a superstar. They both ran and embraced each other. There was such commotion and so much to talk about that they both struggled to have a coherent conversation. The crowds of people who showed up to greet him overwhelmed Shyam. He had spent a lot of time in Lahore, had romanced there, and grew up in Rawalpindi. Lahore, Amritsar, and Rawalpindi were where they had always been, but those days had gone; those nights Shyam had spent there had gone forever, buried anonymously by "the grave diggers of politics." Feeling overly emotional and also a little irritated, Manto left Shyam amidst the throngs of fans after agreeing to meet him at Faletti's Hotel. When Shyam finally came to the hotel and gave an impassioned speech that was enthusiastically received, Manto found it difficult to relate to him. He was especially put off when Shyam asked him to accompany him and others heading to Lahore's red-light district. Manto went home and had several odd dreams, including one in which he told the milkman, "You've completely changed, you bastard, you are a Hindu!" Upon waking up, Manto felt as if had uttered a terrible slur, but he realized that it had not come out of his mouth and was just an effect of the political turmoil of the day. He was glad he had sworn at the milkman in his dream for giving him milk mixed with one quarter of water. Manto felt relieved to think that though Shyam was a Hindu, he was not a Hindu mixed with water![90]

While Manto was a Muslim, his humanity was also not diluted with water, whatever the color or type of cap he chose to wear. Defying the arbitrary frontiers of 1947, he continued to engage with literary personalities in India, commenting on their work and inviting comments on his own. Most of his admirers and supporters in India stuck by him while he was being prosecuted in Pakistan on charges of obscenity. Occasionally the correspondence was disrupted when one or more letters failed to reach its destination. Of those that did arrive, it is worth mentioning one from Amrita Pritam, then in her midthirties, requesting Manto's comments on her novel *Pinjar* (Skeleton). The novel tells of a beautiful young Hindu woman whom a Muslim abducts during the disturbances of 1947 to avenge an old land dispute between their families. Given the nature of the story, Manto in all probability commented favorably on a promising novel that paralleled much of what he had to say about the nature of and motivations behind partition violence, especially against women. Thanking Manto for his letter, Pritam wrote: "It is wonderful that a writer of your merit takes an interest in my work."[91] Manto may well have replied that there was no reason why he should not take an interest in her work. The *batwara*, the word he used for partition, may have divided lives and drawn lines of red in the hearts and minds of sections of the subcontinent's population. But the lines of division drawn by the British were not visible to the eye. They certainly did not extend to the domain of literature, which could never be divided. The pity of partition was not that instead of one country there were now two—independent India and independent Pakistan—but the fact that "human beings in both countries were slaves, slaves of bigotry . . . slaves of religious passions, slaves of animal instincts and barbarity."[92]

III

Histories

"When the Waters Will Flow Again"

Partition: Neither End nor Beginning

"The main newspaper headlines these days are about bloodshed," Manto lamented. He was bewildered by the chaos and confusion attending the dawn of a long-awaited freedom. "Why have human beings become so thirsty for human blood these days?" he asked. "Should we wash our hands of humanity?" "Have we lost faith in that thing called conscience?" He was at a loss as to how to answer these weighty questions. What had happened at the time of partition was a blot on the face of humanity. The unpardonable horrors of partition— women belonging to rival communities being paraded naked; several hundreds of thousands of people killed; and tens of thousands of women raped, maimed, and abducted—ought to have chastened the human instinct for bestiality. Yet there was an unwillingness to outgrow the psychological nightmare of partition. Not a day passed without a human being getting killed by a fellow human being. Scores ended up injured. "Why are these few individuals so murderous," and "why are their hearts and minds so possessed by murder and violence?"[1]

"Something unique and unprecedented had happened."
Concerned as ever with the present, Manto was interested not
in analyzing the causes of partition but in delineating its consequences. By looking at the finer details, all too easily hidden
under loosely defined religious categories, he wanted to tease
out the human impact of partition, something he thought was
ultimately a task for experts in psychology. Taking appropriate
measures could mitigate the pain of partition. "Unfortunately
the concerned parties did not make any honest effort, with
the result that today we see frightening criminals standing
among us." There were no methods in place to reform those
who had become accustomed to the use of knives and guns.
Newspapers were printing stories about the exploits of these
dangerous men and turning them into popular heroes. The
issue of "abducted" women was altogether different. It raised
basic ethical questions. Who would safeguard the bricks in
the buildings supporting these women's yet-to-be-born illegitimate children?[2]

Manto wrote feelingly on the issue of "abducted" women
and their rehabilitation. "When I think of the recovered
women, I think only of their bloated bellies—what will happen to those bellies?" he mused. Would the children of their
misery "belong to Pakistan or Hindustan?" And who would
compensate these women for their nine-month burden, Pakistan or Hindustan? He failed to understand why these women
were called "abducted," a term that to his mind was associated
with romance, in which men and women were equally com-
plicit. What sort of abduction was this in which a defenseless
woman was taken forcibly and locked up? But the times were
such that logic, rationality, and philosophy were useless. It was
like sleeping with the windows and doors closed in the heat

19

Picture of distress—woman consoled by a relative
at the grave of her four-month-old child,
by Margaret Bourke-White, Time & Life Pictures/
Getty Images

of the summer: Manto had shut all the windows and doors
to his heart and mind, even though keeping them open was
more important than ever. "But what could I do, I couldn't
think of anything," he professed. To him the two-way traffic
of abducted women across the newly demarcated borders possessed all the features of a bustling flesh trade.[3] He found it
utterly distasteful that the two governments advertised their

success in recovering these "fallen" women, and he wondered why "we, who keep pets and embrace beasts, cannot give a place to these women and children in our homes." The politicians of both countries needed to answer this before anyone else. "Our split culture and divided civilization, what has survived of our arts; all that we received from the cut-up parts of our own body, and which is buried in the ashes of Western politics, we need to retrieve, dust, clean, and restore to freshness in order to recover all that we have lost in the storm." He thought it imperative to attend to those injuries that could become fatal if left unattended. Of these none was greater than the wounds inflicted on those fifty thousand raped, abducted, and subsequently recovered women, some of these outrages due to "our own cowardice" and others the result of the "unbridled debauchery of our rivals."[4]

Manto's mind was not numbed for long by the human depravity that marked partition. After mingling with the ocean of displaced people huddled in camps across Punjab, he was not only one of the first to address the issue of abducted women; he also questioned commonplace assumptions about partition violence. Manto realized that no more than a few individuals had been involved in the mayhem, which shattered so many worlds in an instant. Without absolving them of their crimes, he believed that the perpetrators of partition violence were a product of a great mishap. They were not habitual killers. Circumstances had turned them into murderers. Like ordinary human beings, they too loved their mothers and friends, protected the honor of their daughters and daughters-in-law, and even had the fear of God in them. All this was blown away by the calamity of partition. Unless the government conducted a psychological study of the growing

Manto arrived in Lahore, via Karachi, around 7 or 8 January 1948 and spent the next three months in a state of agitated confusion. Was he in Bombay, Karachi, or Lahore where musical gatherings were being held at restaurants to collect money for the Quaid-i-Azam Mohammad Ali Jinnah Fund? He felt as if he were watching several films simultaneously—all chaotically interlinked: sometimes it was Bombay's bazaars and backstreets; at others Karachi's fast-moving trams and donkey carts; and, the next moment, Lahore's noisy restaurants. Slouched on a single-seat sofa at 31 Lakshmi Mansions, lost in thought, Manto was shaken out of his slumber once the money he had brought from Bombay ran out. He knew then that he was in Lahore, where he had come periodically for his court cases and bought beautiful shoes. How was he going to make a living here? Lahore's film industry was paralyzed. Film companies had no existence beyond signboards. The race for allotments of properties abandoned by Hindus and Sikhs was the only game in town, but Manto could not bring himself to partake of the loot bazaar. The poets Faiz Ahmad Faiz and Chiragh Hasan Hasrat drew him to writing for the daily *Imroze*. Mentally perturbed, Manto could not decide what to write about. "Despite trying, I could not separate India from Pakistan and Pakistan from India." He had innumerable questions and no obvious answers. In what ways would Pakistani literature be distinctive? Who owned the literature written in undivided India? Would it be divided as well? Weren't the basic problems confronting Indians and Pakistanis the same? Was Urdu going to become extinct in India, and what shape would it assume in Pakistan? "Will our state be a religious state?" Manto wondered. "We will of course always remain loyal to the state, but will we be allowed to criticize the gov-

20
Manto in Lahore, no date

ernment?" And, above all else, "Will independence make the circumstances here different from what they were in the colonial era?"[6]

These fundamental questions about the nature of the postcolonial transition have continued to resonate in the public discourse of the subcontinent. They also were the inspiration for my own historical inquiry into the causes and consequences of India's partition. The literary presence of the conspicuously absent Manto Abajan—literally, father, as I grew up calling my great-uncle while living in Lakshmi Mansions and beyond—had a subtle role to play in the making of this historian. I grew up knowing the grim nuances of several of his partition stories. I was especially proud to have memorized the gibberish—"Upar the gur gur the annexe the bay dhayana the moong the dal of the laltain"—uttered by the main character in the highly acclaimed story "Toba Tek Singh."[7] Manto's stories about the human degeneracy that marked independence and the birth of Pakistan, whether in the form of rapes, abductions, or murders, instilled in me a desire to gauge the extent to which they were actually corroborated by the historical evidence. I was also keen to probe the self-definition of the new state that emerged out of the partition process, and which persecuted Manto on charges of obscenity when he wrote about the experience of raped and abducted women.

Partition was both the central historical event in twentieth-century South Asia and a historical process that has continued unfolding to this day. It is common to hear in the subcontinent that the most pressing problems besetting India, Pakistan, and Bangladesh today have their origin in the decisions of expediency taken in 1947. An exploration of Manto's life and literature provides the historian with a novel way to address the complex relationship between the event and the processes of partition. Hailed as a keen observer of the moment of partition, Manto was equally, if not more powerfully, an astute narrator of its continuing aftershocks. His corpus of writings in multiple genres during the first seven years of postcolonial Pakistan offers historians a range of resources to reconnect the histories of individuals, families, communities, and the state.

The growing availability of his short stories in translation in different languages, notably English, Hindi, and Japanese, has made Manto increasingly more accessible to a global reading public. Although he is acclaimed for his nonjudgmental portrayal of prostitutes and a plethora of other socially taboo subjects, Manto's international reputation as a short story writer has for the most part rested on his gripping narratives of partition. An exclusive emphasis on Manto as a realistic short story writer has tended to deflect attention from his other no-less-significant writings. The previous chapter delineated the value of his personality sketches as a means for the historical retrieval of different kinds of individual and collective memory. He was a prolific essayist as well and wrote on a wide spectrum of burning social issues—a corpus that places him among the all-time leading public intellectuals of South Asia, if such a category could be deemed to exist in the aftermath of 1947. Not as well known as Manto's stories, the biting social critiques in his essays lend themselves well to the writing of histories, not just of the long postcolonial transition. They are also important sources for the historian of Cold War era politics, and of the cultural and intellectual implications of the Pakistani state's efforts to project an Islamic identity to exert an artificial sense of homogeneity within and distinctiveness without, notably in relation to India.

Manto's popularity on both sides of the borders drawn in 1947 makes him an especially valuable source for the historian. With his no-holds-barred critique of society and his unshakable belief in the inherent goodness of people, however lowly and despicable they may seem to others, he makes the postcolonial moment come alive in all its ambivalences and contradictions. Accessible to a broad readership without slipping into shallowness or superficialities, he is a realist painter rather than a photographer in his depiction of partition. He saw partition not simply as an event tossing on the surface of the waves that the strong tides of history carry on their backs, to borrow a phrase from the French historian Fernand

were flowing side by side, one of life and the other of death. Manto met his old friends Ahmad Nadeem Qasimi and Sahir Ludhianvi and found them to be as disorientated and mentally incapacitated as he was. So he started loitering about on the streets, silently listening to what others were saying. Gradually the weight lifted from his mind, and he decided to write light and humorous essays for *Imroze*. Soon he was composing fast-paced and sarcastic pieces that were much appreciated and later published in a collection named *Talkh, Tursh aur Shireen* (Bitter, Acrimonious, and Sweet).[9]

Manto still could not bring himself to return to writing fiction. He considered the short story to be a "very grave" genre. Pressed by Ahmad Nadeem Qasimi to write a story for his newly launched journal *Naqoosh*, Manto procrastinated until their friendship was on the line. To please Qasimi, he wrote his first short story in Pakistan, "Thanda Gosht" (Colder than Ice). Set against the backdrop of partition violence in Punjab, it is a chilling drama about an illiterate and hypersexed Sikh, Ishwar Singh, who becomes impotent, to the chagrin of his oversexed partner, Kalwant Kaur, after a psychologically crippling incident. An active participant in the disturbances, he kidnaps a beautiful teenage Muslim girl after killing half a dozen members of her family. Flinging the girl over his shoulder, Ishwar Singh heads toward the city canal near the railway tracks, lays her down under some bushes, and is about to force himself on her when he is shaken to the core to discover that she has already died out of sheer terror. Ishwar Singh is in acute emotional agony, not because he has killed innocent people but because he cannot get over the girl's cold flesh. Faced with his lover's jealousy, he tells her the painful story with teary eyes, and suddenly dies—his hands colder than ice.[10]

Qasimi liked the story but declined to publish it, fearing it was too hot for *Naqoosh*, a collaborative endeavor he had initiated with the board for the promotion of Urdu in Pakistan. Manto took back the story quietly and told him to come back the next evening. When Qasimi returned the next day, Manto was writing the climax of "Khol Du" (Open It). Qasimi had to wait a long time, as Manto took extra care in writing the crucial final lines of the story. Based on partition violence, like "Thanda Gosht," "Khol Du" is the story of Sirajuddin, a Muslim father frantically looking for his kidnapped daughter, Sakina. A group of eight young Muslim men working as volunteers in the refugee camps offer to help him locate her. On finding Sakina, they gang-rape her and leave her lying unconscious near the railroad tracks. She is taken to a camp hospital, where Sirajuddin eventually finds her, lying motionless like a corpse. When a doctor comes in and feels the girl's pulse, he motions toward the window and tells Sirajuddin, "Open it." Upon hearing the doctor's words, the half-dead Sakina responds mechanically, opening the knot of her trousers and pushing them down her thighs. Sirajuddin's wrinkled face lights up as he cries, "My daughter's alive"; the doctor breaks into a sweat.[11] Demolishing the myth of religiously motivated violence, the story tears at the heart and silently jeers at the unquestioned idioms of statist nationalism. Manto watched Qasimi quiver as he read the last lines before mustering the energy to say, "It's good . . . I'll take it."[12] "If someone other than Manto had been sitting next to me," Qasimi recalled, "I would have wept out loud." Putting the story into his pocket, he told himself that if "Khol Du" was declared obscene, short story writers should quit the profession and take on some useful job.[13]

"Khol Du" was published in *Naqoosh*'s third number in August 1948. Much appreciated by literary connoisseurs, it generated commotion in government circles, where it was deemed to be a threat to the preservation of public peace. *Naqoosh* was banned for six months, an action that was bitterly criticized in the press and elicited protest from the Progressive Writers Association, but to no avail. Manto had announced his arrival in Pakistan with aplomb. There was to be no turning back. After a few days the editor of another progressive journal, *Adab-i-Latif,* came to see Manto and took away the manuscript of "Thanda Gosht." The story was ready for publication when it caught someone's eye and was immediately stopped from going into print. Following two successive attempts to bring it out, Manto included "Thanda Gosht" in a collection of his short stories entitled *Nimrood ki Khudai* (Nimrod's Godliness). Just then Arif Abdul Mateen, the editor of a brand-new journal, *Javed*—owned by Nasir Anwar, who was to become a very close family friend—started badgering Manto to let him print "Thanda Gosht." Manto resisted but then gave in, scribbling a chit to his publisher withdrawing the story, commenting that the management of *Javed* wanted to get their journal proscribed. The story was duly published in *Javed*'s special number in March 1949 and distributed throughout the subcontinent. A month went by uneventfully. That was too good to be true. The Press Branch was still under the control of an old tormentor of Manto's, Chaudhry Mohammad Hussain, who, despite being old and frail, had the power to set the police machinery moving with great force. *Javed*'s office was ransacked and all the available copies confiscated. Nasir Anwar sent a note to Manto with the bad news, adding, "You should go back to where you were acquitted of the charges three times; I think this will be the last time."[14]

The case was brought before the Press Advisory Board, whose convener, Faiz Ahmad Faiz, was the editor of the then progressive *Pakistan Times*. Left to himself, Faiz would have promptly dismissed the charges of obscenity brought against "Thanda Gosht." But the panel deciding the case included die-hard conservatives, who ranted against both Manto's story and *Javed*'s rebellious disposition. When Faiz defended "Thanda Gosht," Maulana Akhtar Ali, who had replaced his esteemed father, Maulana Zafar Ali Khan, as editor of *Zamindar*, roared: "No, no, this sort of literature will not work in Pakistan." This sentiment was heartily endorsed by other conservatives on the panel. The real howler came from the irrepressible Chaudhry Mohammad Hussain, the hard-nosed former watchdog of the colonial state's censorship network and now the self-appointed guardian of the newly created Muslim postcolonial state. Summarizing the story for the English editor of the *Civil and Military Gazette*, Hussain expressed outrage that the central message of "Thanda Gosht" was that "we Muslims are so dishonorable that the Sikhs did not even spare one of our dead girls."[15] Arguing against this line of attack was pointless, and so the matter had to be left for the deliberation of the courts.

Manto had seen it all before and, like his own character Ustad Mangu, could not discern that the winning of freedom had altered the atmosphere in any way at the Lahore District Courts. Words could not describe them. They were as filthy and murky as ever. Things moved ever so slowly and painfully. Absolutely nothing had changed. Manto was once again in the dock under the exact same colonial laws of obscenity, now section 292 C of the Pakistani Penal Code. Familiar questions were raised about the relationship between literature and ethics, and about art as a reflection of real life versus art as social criticism, and by and large the same sorts of answers given. The usual suspects appeared for the prosecution and the defense. Dyed-in-the-wool traditionalists, such as Maulana Ihsanullah Khan Tajwar Najibabadi and Agha Hashar Kashmiri, made the case for the prosecution, while progressives of varying hues and colors, like Faiz Ahmad Faiz, Khalifa Abdul Hakim, and Sufi Ghulam Mustapha Tabassum, came forward on behalf of the defense. The one heartwarming moment for Manto during the entire ordeal occurred when, after he had been forsaken by his lawyer, four young attorneys walked into the courtroom out of the blue and offered him their services.[16] This was an indication of the chasm between the literalist attitudes of those in the state bureaucracy, on one hand, and, on the other, the element of public opinion that agreed with Manto's contention that "Thanda Gosht," far from being obscene, was a reformist story.

As was to be expected, Manto authored his own best defense, which the rather ill-tempered and opinionated magistrate Mian A. M. Saeed thought was sufficient in itself to convict him. Manto used the example of Gustave Flaubert's defense lawyer, who successfully defended the French author against obscenity charges for *Madame Bovary* (1857) by arguing that his client had written a serious and sad book after extensive research and thought. "Thanda Gosht" too was a serious story, saturated with melancholy. The story was far from being even remotely obscene; rather, Manto thought it was extremely healthy that its writer had not lost faith in humanity. "I am sorry that a piece of writing telling human beings that they are not separated from humanity even when they become animal-like should be considered obscene and sexually suggestive," Manto wrote. What could be more wonderfully paradoxical than the fact that Ishwar Singh's own residual humanity punishes him most severely? Anyone offended by the story needed to seek psychiatric help because, as he had said while defending himself in the face of obscenity charges against the story "Dhuan" (Smoke), only a sick mind could interpret such things in the wrong way. Manto referred to the obscenity charges brought against James Joyce for *Ulysses.* The American judge who acquitted Joyce noted that courts could decide whether or not a work of literature was obscene by the impact it had on ordinary people. Poets wrote poetry, writers wrote stories, and painters made paintings, for those who were mentally and physically healthy. "My stories are for healthy people, normal human beings," Manto exclaimed, "not for minds who dig up carnal meanings in innocent and pure things." He had given a true picture in "Thanda Gosht" and exposed a psychological reality. If the story had vulgar language, it reflected the mental state of the characters uttering it, and not that of the author. He concluded by regretting that the prosecution had not said anything about the story from a literary perspective. If they had criticized the technical flaws of the story, he would have been delighted. Instead he had been made to stand in the dock like an ordinary criminal on the demeaning charge of stirring people's sexual desires.[17]

On 16 January 1950 the trial court's verdict pronounced Manto guilty of obscenity. He was sentenced to three months of "rigorous imprisonment" (hard labor) and fined three hundred rupees. The nonpayment of the fine carried an additional twenty-one days in prison. The editor and publisher of

actual state of our society . . . as we have obviously not yet attained our ideal." How could Manto's story be considered obscene when journalism and publishing, as well as the cinema, were heavily imbued with Western culture? "Kissing and hugging is something which is depicted in the cinema daily." Adultery was the "main plot of all the English and Western novels." "If no objection is raised to these," the judge asserted, "I see no reason why we should be hard upon these young men." He had read "Thanda Gosht" and found some "vulgar and indecent" language of the kind that is "common in our ordinary, low society." While he did not "approve" of the story, the judge also did "not consider it 'obscene' or so very objectionable to condemn it as such." A significant feature of the judgment, and one in keeping with the ruling on Joyce's *Ulysses* in America, was that the question of a work's obscenity could not be decided by experts and depended on its impact on the general readership. On this view the expert evidence collected by the trial court was inadmissible and could at best be treated as ordinary opinion on whether or not "Thanda Gosht" ran afoul of accepted notions of decency in society.[19] Matters did not end there, as the government appealed the decision, which was upheld on 18 April 1952. Manto and the others had to pay a fine of three hundred rupees each to avoid serving one month in prison.

Throughout the trial Manto had consistently argued that the very title of the story, emphasizing deathlike coldness, showed that his intention was not to arouse carnal passions. Letters from a cross section of people throughout the subcontinent reveal that the claim was endorsed in the court of public opinion. A lowly civil servant in the Punjab government's auditor general's office, who was not a writer, a college graduate, or the son of a rich man, thought Manto's proscribed short stories "Thanda Gosht" and "Khol Du" were most effective and socially meaningful. Though he did not possess a bush shirt or crepe-soled shoes—the mark of a well-heeled man— Kausar Anwari aspired to become acquainted with "the great writer targeted for obscenity and ethical perversion," because Manto's fearless individuality in the world of literature was like "a rock that could withstand the mightiest of storms."[20]

In a profoundly perceptive letter from Mysore, Mir Tajammul Hussain expressed surprise that Manto had been booked for "Thanda Gosht" and "Khol Du" despite his persuasive and well-publicized defense against accusations of obscenity brought by the colonial state on three previous occasions. Of the two postpartition stories, Hussain had read only "Thanda Gosht." While it might not be one of Manto's best short stories, Hussain wrote, it could be considered to be among the best Urdu short stories and was certainly more meaningful than several emotionally charged writings in that genre. The conclusion left such a lasting impression that, with one stroke of the pen, Manto had taken the art of short story writing to new heights. Issues of sexuality had been raised because they were intrinsic to the story. However, they were addressed with such artistic mastery that instead of becoming coarsely sexually aroused, the reader was absorbed by the "suspense" created by the author and wanted only to know "what will happen next." Given that the importance of sexuality was universally recognized, it seemed unconscionable to penalize artists for bringing it up, especially when the subject was introduced with good intentions. Just as only an extraordinary mind could create the characters of "Thanda Gosht," a healthy mind was needed to grasp the significance of showing that even a reprobate like Ishwar Singh was not altogether devoid of humanity. Far from being vulgar or obscene, the story demonstrated the depth of Manto's human sympathies and was infinitely better than the artificial and unnatural yarns written for the sake of fortune and fame. Those who condemned "Thanda Gosht" and its writer for obscenity were in fact giving expression to their own guilty conscience. In Hussain's opinion, Manto was unique because—unlike other writers, who found gloom in broad daylight—he looked for flashes of light in the depths of darkness and felt greater pain for human beings than even Krishan Chander.[21]

There was jubilation among Manto's friends and well-wishers on both sides of the border after his acquittal on obscenity charges for "Thanda Gosht." Balwant Singh Gargi, with whom he had spent time at All-India Radio in New Delhi, wrote, congratulating him on his feat.[22] "Your victory is for the betterment of literature, how can a donkey know the value of saffron?" wrote an unknown admirer, Mahmud Saleem, from the backwaters of Gujranwala, just over forty miles north of Lahore. Those who filed cases against Manto were hypocrites trying to avoid correcting the sins of their own flesh.[23] Letters and telegrams came from all parts of Pakistan, including the NWFP and East Bengal, saluting his unshakable courage and literary skills. Those with literary ambitions of their own requested that, as the country's leading short story writer, he ought to consider placing them under his mentorship. Regardless of the view in certain quarters, the taint of obscenity did not stick; if anything, it even served to enhance Manto's reputation.

This is not to say that ordinary people did not take him to task for writing about awkward and unspeakable things, invariably generalizing what Manto had deliberately individualized. The personalized reaction to "Khol Du" from a young college student named Khalid, who had served as a volunteer in the refugee camps, makes the point. He accepted the validity of what Manto had written and respected him as a good artist. But what Manto had said was not true of all the volunteers. During his summer vacations Khalid had led a group of thirteen volunteers in the Chinese Barracks camp from 18 August to 29 September 1947. None of the young men he worked with was remotely capable of the "dirty mindedness" displayed by the volunteers in "Khol Du." While he did not want to sound boastful, Khalid was proud to say that he looked upon the refugee women at the camp as he did his mother and sisters, and deemed it wrong to take even a mouthful of the food assigned to them. He was prepared to accept that some volunteers might have been like the characters in Manto's story. However, this did not mean that they all had the same mentality. It saddened Khalid to think that a writer of Manto's stature had such contempt for the volunteers, when most of them had performed their tasks selflessly and honestly. He wanted to know why Manto had formed such a lowly opinion of these servants of humanity.[24] Manto may well have written back and said that to read "Khol Du" as a condemnation of all volunteers was as erroneous as dignifying them all with the highest moral virtues as Khalid, in his desire for self-justification, was prepared to do.

Concerned with stretching, not shrinking, the psychological canvas displaying the multifaceted influences on human behavior, Manto was up against much more than personal hubris. Ideological orientations that limited individual freedom of expression, and were pure anathema to him, were for many of his literary associates a matter of not just intellectual principles but also social necessity. What hurt him more than the obvious inconveniences of prosecution under the postcolonial state's censorship laws was the doctrinaire attitude of the self-styled progressive writers, and most egregiously of his friend Ahmad Nadeem Qasimi. Manto was never a member of the Progressive Writers Association (PWA), the vanguard of a left-oriented anti-imperialist movement in Urdu literature influenced by radical literary avant-garde trends during the interwar years in Europe, most notably in Britain. The PWA emerged out of the controversy generated by the publication in 1932 of *Angarey* (Burning Embers), a collection of nine short stories and one drama by four English-educated urban middle-class Muslims—Sajjad Zaheer, Ahmed Ali, Rasheed Jehan, and Mahmud-ul-Zafar. With the exception of Ahmed Ali, the rest were communist sympathizers and were linked with *ashraf* (respectable) society in Lucknow, a key center of Urdu-speaking culture. The outrage expressed in conservative Urdu newspapers and journals of the city against *Angarey*'s blistering critique of North Indian Muslim society's sexual, religious, and political mores led to its proscription in 1933 by the colonial government of the United Provinces. This prompted the formation in 1935, in a central London Chinese restaurant, of the Indian Progressive Writers Association by a group of Indian writers led by *Angarey*'s editor, Sajjad Zaheer.[25]

As much as he shared the PWA's contempt for the hollow moral values of urban Muslim middle-class *ashraf* society, Manto could not accept its stern opposition to the notion of literature for literature's sake. More irksome was the PWA's insistence that literature could be socially meaningful only if it depicted the real-life struggles of laborers and peasants—an unthinkable limitation for the maverick in him. The ultimate jolt came in 1945 when the PWA, meeting in Hyderabad, adopted a resolution condemning obscenity in literature, just when Manto and Ismat Chughtai were being harassed by the colonial courts.[26] Manto had been thinking of revolutionary change before Sajjad Zaheer or anyone of his ilk appeared on the literary stage pronouncing radical socialist transformation. He was also writing on many of the themes the progressive writers condoned. This explains why, despite disagreeing on what modern literature should or should not represent, Manto had been able to forge meaningful bonds with hardline PWA affiliates. These included the likes of Ismat Chughtai, Rajinder Singh Bedi, and Sardar Jafri, to say nothing of Qasimi, who instigated the long-drawn-out quarrel between Manto and the progressive writers in the postcolonial era.

The sole cause of the estrangement was Manto's decision to join hands with the literary critic Mohammad Hasan Askari to launch *Urdu Adab* in June 1948, with the cooperation of Lahore's Maktaba-i-Jadid press. An individualist and nonconformist like Manto, Askari had been denounced as a conservative "reactionary" and a mouthpiece of the Pakistani state by the PWA. The denunciation was prompted by Askari's efforts to facilitate the postcolonial project of promoting the Islamic basis of Pakistani culture. In 1948 the PWA had gone so far as to say that a non-Marxist could not be a "progressive," an intellectually stifling criterion that excluded not just Askari but other trailblazers of modern literature like Manto and Rajinder Singh Bedi. Opposed to the growing cliquishness of progressive writers, Manto actually valued Askari's contributions to modernist Urdu literature. His farsightedness has to be acknowledged. Askari is now regarded as one of the all-time leading critics of modern Urdu literature.[27]

Matters had been coming to a head since Manto asked Askari to write the introduction to his partition sketches, *Siyah Hashiye* (Black Margins), published in 1948 by Maktaba-i-Jadid. In September 1948, Qasimi took the extraordinary step of writing an open letter to Manto, expressing shock and disdain for his association with Askari. As he explained in an interview later, Manto's old friends disliked Askari's fondness for the French school of thought represented by Jean-Paul Sartre, André Gide, and others. "We thought Askari was an escapist and was ruining Manto," Qasimi declared. Upon hearing others speak of the letter, Manto came to see Qasimi and said: "Why do you write open letters to me? I will write a closed letter to you." But after reading the letter, Manto was, according to Qasimi, "very happy because there was nothing derogatory in it about his personality or his art." Qasimi had missed the point of Manto's barb about retaliating with a closed letter. Manto came to see Qasimi again and said that while the letter was acceptable, "these things should be talked over among friends rather than published in a magazine."[28]

Ali Sardar Jafri, who wrote the introduction to Manto's collection of short stories *Chugad*, published from Bombay in 1948, had tried warning him. Accusing Askari of plagiarizing European literature, Sardar Jafri called him a "fundamentalist" and an enemy of progress. Jafri had differences with both Manto and Ismat but respected them, whereas he considered Askari unconscionable.[29] A month before Qasimi aired the grievance publicly, Sardar Jafri again wrote to Manto, saying he had recently pilloried Askari for writing an objectionable article. "We are all worried here" because "there is no match between you and Askari."[30] When the government of Pakistan banned *Naqoosh* and *Sawera*, edited by Qasimi, as well as Manto's and Askari's joint venture, *Urdu Adab*, for six months, Sardar Jafri was dismayed. It was an intolerable situation, tantamount to "animosity toward literature and an attack on culture in order to uphold the coercive power of capitalism." There could be no free literature or free society under such conditions. He could do nothing sitting in India but had high expectations of Manto's pen. "Let them ban every story," Sardar Jafri exploded, applauding Manto's gumption and stating his desire to emulate him.[31] Jafri considered "Khol Du" to be a "masterpiece of the era" and urged Manto to send him a story, preferably on abducted women, for his journal *Naya Adab* (New Literature).[32] The affection and warmth in Jafri's tone was soon to change. Manto, for his part, did not send him anything for *Naya Adab*, mainly because of the difficulties he was facing in getting royalty payments from India. After reading the introduction to *Siyah Hashiye*, which he found highly objectionable, Jafri was at a loss to understand Manto's love affair with Askari. Anyone who could write a laudatory introduction, as Askari had done, for a book by a literary dinosaur like M. Aslam had to be dishonest. Worse still, Askari had become the official Pakistani scribe. It was regrettable that Manto's name now would be uttered in the same breath as that of M. Aslam.[33]

Agitated by Manto's refusal to correct his course, the PWA formally adopted a resolution blacklisting him as a reactionary writer. Ostracism is emotionally difficult to bear even in the best of circumstances. Still struggling to earn a reasonable income in Pakistan, Manto now could no longer publish his writings in journals and newspapers controlled by the progres-

sive writers. The blacklisting also explains Ahmad Nadeem
Qasimi's absence from the scene after the autumn of 1948 and
the rather lukewarm support offered to Manto by Faiz Ahmad
Faiz and other progressive writers during the "Thanda Gosht"
trial. While not endorsing the state prosecution's charges of
obscenity, progressive writers in Pakistan and India did precious little to come to the defense of someone they had considered one of their own and had now declared a reactionary,
with no reference whatsoever to the actual facts. Exemplifying
this distorted perception were the unfounded fears of the progressive writers that *Urdu Adab* would become a hotbed of
reaction and statist ideas if Manto brought it out with Askari.
Condemned at its conception and banned after its first publication, the journal appeared only once more. Yet in bringing together prominent writers from both sides of the freshly
demarcated frontier, the two issues occupy a special place in
postindependence Urdu literature in the subcontinent.[34]

Even his supposed "enemy" Upendranath Ashk wrote
from Allahabad and promised to send something for a journal he had not seen. He had no doubt that it would be "very
good" if Manto was bringing it out. Less dogmatic than
other progressive writers, Ashk was prepared to forgo monetary payment for the story if *Urdu Adab* was Manto's own
venture, adding that it would allow him to return to Urdu,
from which he had grown distant of late.[35] Reacting to the
negative publicity given to *Urdu Adab* by would-be progressives and state censors alike, an ordinary reader applauded
the efforts of its editors in no uncertain terms. Setting the
record straight, he declared the journal to be a "milestone"
in the history of the Urdu literary tradition. It was the only
publication of its kind in the entire subcontinent that was

uality, labor rights, and other distasteful aspects of life. He and others were wrongly called progressives, pornographers, and lovers of labor. It was also said that these writers were obsessed with women. Men had obsessed over women since the days of Adam. "And why not?" Manto asked. "Should men be obsessed with elephants and horses?" So long as a thick wall separated men and women emotionally, Ismat Chughtai would continue scratching its cement with her sharp nails. Speaking for himself, Manto denied he was a troublemaker. He did not want to create commotion in people's minds and hearts. "How could I expose the bosom of society when it was already naked?" People called him a "black pen," but he wrote with white chalk on a black slate so that its blackness could become more visible and known. That for him constituted the real meaning of progress.[37]

Manto chose not to formally respond to Qasimi's open letter, but he hammered the dubious politics of his former progressive allies in introductions to two of his short story collections. For an opening salvo, he dropped Ali Sardar Jafri's brief introduction for the Pakistani edition of *Chugad*. Manto explained that he had not done this out of any personal grudge against Jafri or because he had started hating him. But in light of the meaningless furor over his "reactionary" writings in Bombay's so-called progressive circles, of which Jafri was a leading member, it was the only appropriate thing to do. When one of the stories in the anthology, "Babu Gopinath," first came out, the progressive writers, including Jafri, Ismat Chughtai, and Krishan Chander, had acclaimed it. Now progressive writers in India and Pakistan were attacking the same story as reactionary, unethical, and abhorrent. Much the same kind of treatment was being meted out to his other stories, which had earlier been praised lavishly. Referring to his correspondence with Sardar Jafri, Manto marveled at the pace of communications between groups of progressive writers inhabiting the two estranged subcontinental neighbors. News from the backwaters of Pakistan reached the Kremlin and Bombay within seconds and was so reliable that *Siyah Hashiye* had been consigned to the rubbish bin of progressive politics even before it saw the light of day. Manto thought it a delicious irony that while he was being blackballed as a reactionary, an individualist, and a hedonist by the progressive writers, one of their main representative organs, the journal *Sawera* (Dawn), had come out with a completely over-the-top advertisement for one of his books. He was described as a "paragon of honesty," who wielded the double-edged sword of truth mercilessly to cut down the thick jungles hiding the artificiality rampant in state and society. "When abused, Manto smiled; caring nothing for prayers and punishments he was following a path on which only he could walk." Laughing aloud, Manto retorted: "These self-styled progressives and their progressive publishers are so devoid of conscience that they had struck a course on which they alone could walk." If they burned all the books of the blacklisted reactionaries, he would "kiss their hands." Manto had nothing against the progressives, but the careless twisting and turning of the so-called progressives did get to him.[38]

Hauled over the coals by the postcolonial state for exposing the morally repugnant aspects of life, and boycotted by his intellectual peers for unscrupulous reasons, Manto became steadily more frustrated, lonely, angry, and embittered. Instead of just drinking excessively, he now started living to drink. He wrote stories primarily to buy the poor-quality brew that was locally available, and, as he confessed, expediting the slow death that was life. The introduction to his collection of short stories *Yazid* is a mirror of his mental state three and a half years after he moved to Pakistan. Defending his partition sketches, *Siyah Hashiye*, Manto described his endeavor in highly emotional terms: "I dived into the ocean of blood that flows in the veins of human beings and selected a few pearls of the efforts made by man in spilling his brother's last drop of blood, of the tears that flowed in anguish from the eyes of some people who could not suspend their humanity . . . it was these pearls that I presented." "I am a human being," he continued, "and have all the weaknesses and strengths that are in other human beings." "Believe me, I was saddened, very saddened, when a few of my associates raised objections about my efforts, called me a humorist, cynic, inappropriate and reactionary." Alluding to Qasimi, Manto regretted that one of his dear friends had savaged his partition sketches in public, when private criticism might have sufficed. Manto was especially agitated by Qasimi's allegation that he had crafted his partition sketches by collecting cigarette butts, rings, and such things out of the pockets of the dead. "I am a human being and I was angry," Manto admitted. He wanted to give a fitting response to the filth thrown at him. But he desisted and thought silence was best:

> I was angry, not because "A" had misinterpreted me. I was angry because "A" had questioned my intentions only as a fad by clutching at the finger of an infirm and barren movement inspired by the false honor of an external politics and assessed me against a measure in which "red" alone was gold.[39]

Manto had contempt for the progressive writers whose manifestos and resolutions were relayed from the Kremlin to Bombay and then onwards to the Lahore office of the Communist Party on McLeod Road. Some Russian writer or intellectual was constantly being cited. It infuriated him that these progressives did not speak about the part of the world where they lived and breathed. "If we have stopped producing intellectuals," he asked, "did the remedy for this sterility lie in red insemination?" He was angry because in the mad scramble for properties and power no one paid any heed to issues that really mattered. What sort of a government would there be in Pakistan? What would be the relationship of the individual and the party with the state and the government? These were vital questions that required serious thought. Unfortunately the so-called intellectuals were in a hurry to grab the leadership of some organization or another. The custodians of progressive literature first decided that no member of their party would work or write for an official paper. Manto was emphatically opposed to placing unnecessary hurdles in the way of struggling artists looking for jobs. Such a policy smacked of distrust on the part of the progressive writers for their members and, in any case, was something for the government to be concerned about. In time, progressive writers were barred from government-controlled newspapers and radio stations. Government, which was the other name of folly, had even started putting progressive writers behind bars. Manto was sorry that the government and the progressive writers were both victims of an inferiority complex. He was sorrier for the progressive writers who were playing politics with literature at the Kremlin's behest.[40]

Otherwise reasonable people were refusing to have any truck with the state for ideological reasons, overlooking the fact that struggling to feed the stomach was the single most important part of the human endeavor. Accused of being "a pornographer, terrorist, cynic, humorist, and a reactionary," he was in fact a husband and father of three daughters and had to provide for his family. Some of his friends were much worse off, and it distressed him not to be able to help them. What caused him greater consternation was the thought that after his death his writings might become widely accessible and acquire the same revered status as Iqbal's poetry. By contrast, the treatment he was currently receiving was a pleasant experience: "May God protect me from the termites who will chew on my dry bones in the grave!" Manto got depressed when he heard that literature was stagnant or in decline. This was similar to talk about "Islam in danger." Literature was a force like Islam and could never stagnate. It was "our stagnation and decline that we project on literature." Literature and politics had to be kept on separate tracks, as they had distinctive goals. Literature was not someone's monopoly that could be contracted out. Utterly dismayed by the state of affairs, Manto stated:

> Earlier I was accepted as a progressive and later suddenly turned into a reactionary. Now the fatwa givers were thinking of once again reclaiming me as a progressive, and the state that gave its own fatwas on fatwas considered me a progressive, i.e., a red. . . . a communist, and, sometimes out of exasperation, a pornographer and tried me in court. Yet this same state's publications advertised that "Saadat Hasan Manto is our country's great author and short story writer whose pen has remained active during the recent turbulent times." . . . my sad heart shiv-

ers at the thought that this fickle-minded state may be pleased to hang a medal on my coffin, which would be a great insult to me.[41]

Manto's conscience was not for sale, however hard he had to strive to make money through his writings. Mohammad Hasan Askari, whose friendship exposed him to the fury of the progressive writers, considered Manto's struggle to survive as an artist to be intrinsic to Pakistan's immediate postindependence history. They first met about eight months after partition. Writers were still finding it difficult to come to terms with the unexpected creation of Pakistan and debating how to make it a part of their literary repertoire. Incapable of denying what was concrete, Manto accepted the reality of Pakistan and brought it within the ambit of his literary production, not because he was a reactionary or participating in a statist conspiracy. Adaptable to change, he experimented with the new without ever considering the attempt to be complete. Manto liked looking at things from different angles. This was what brought him into conflict with those—whether progressive writers, Pakistan's state managers, or seekers of power in general—who wanted artists to produce the kind of art that they deemed to be opportune or expedient at any given time. The problem was universal and not limited to Pakistan. Many artists succumbed to such pressures, but there were those like Manto who were mentally and spiritually incapable of accepting dictation in conducting their creative experiments. Nonconformists did not pretend to be leaders of humanity or bearers of truth; there was no time to make self-serving claims when one was engrossed in portraying the experiences of life in as balanced a way as possible, regardless of whether that hurt or benefited anyone. "In our country there is one such man, Manto, and since there is none like him within sight, the importance of his mental struggle in our eyes becomes even more significant." Askari concluded with a telling couplet: "For God's sake do not stop him; he is the only killer left in the city."[42]

Blacklisted by the progressives, prosecuted by the state, and maligned by the right-wing media, Manto left no stone unturned to make the most of his decision to move to Pakistan. The Halqa-i-Arbab-i-Zauq (Circle of People with Good Taste), a modern literary movement started in 1936—which, unlike the PWA, was apolitical—provided an outlet for his stifled intellectual energies and helped satisfy the need for public appreciation. He had always been deeply interested in the different dialects of the Punjabi language, which he spoke at home as well as in the company of friends. Among his early ventures was the script of a Punjabi film *Baeli* (Belle), directed by his nephew Masud Pervez and financed by some members of the Manto family, including his sister Iqbal. Released in 1950, the movie flopped at the box office, putting an end to Manto's hopes of working for Pakistan's ill-equipped film industry.[43] The abysmal failure of *Baeli* meant that no producer would risk offering him a writing job. The timing was particularly unfortunate, as his friend Shaukat Hussain Rizvi and his talented wife, Noor Jahan, had just started the Shahnoor Studio on Lahore's Multan Road after a self-imposed break of three years following partition. Manto tried his hand at filmmaking in Pakistan for the second and last time with *Doosri Kothi* (Other Bungalow), which was also a failure. He now had no choice but to rely exclusively on his short stories and essays for a livelihood. Despite the draconian restrictions on where he could publish, and the lethal effects of consuming large quantities of toxic alcohol, Manto managed to earn more money from literature than any other Urdu writer of his age. His productivity in the period following partition was nothing short of remarkable. Between 1948 and 1951 he published seven anthologies of short stories and wrote innumerable essays. In October 1950 he assumed editorial responsibility for the Lahore weekly *Nigarash*, which published light literary and satirical pieces on a range of contemporary issues, including the Kashmir dispute, Pakistan's foreign policy, and culture. Manto authored most of them, under a pseudonym, as few writers wanted to risk associating with an individual who raised hackles on both extremes of the political spectrum. It was a short-lived enterprise, adding to Manto's accumulated disappointments and mounting despair.

According to a close observer of Manto's descent into the whirlpool of self-annihilation, "to earn more he had to write more, to write more he felt he must have more of his self prescribed tonic, the more he drank the less he wrote, the less he wrote the more worried he became, the more worried he became the more he drank to forget his worries."[44] Living among extended family in Lahore may have made him more irresponsible than he was in Bombay, where he had taken the precaution of getting a life insurance policy. Manto was a genuinely caring husband and compassionate father, but his professional disillusionments in Pakistan turned his domestic life into a living hell for Safia. She considered leaving him, only to be persuaded by her family to make the most of a bad situation. One day he voluntarily agreed to try and kick the habit. The only treatment for alcoholism available was in the Punjab Mental Hospital's antialcoholic ward in Lahore. On 25 April 1951 he

21
Safia with sister Zakia,
by Brij Mohan, Bombay,
1947

was admitted to the hospital, which led to a wildfire of rumors across the subcontinent that Manto had gone insane. He was released on 2 June 1951 and abstained from drinking for some months. It was the "most productive period" of his life, during which he wrote a book a month, at the rate of one story each day. His so-called friends did not allow this phase to last for long. He started drinking again and, on 27 December 1951, was forcibly readmitted to the mental hospital by his family. On 9 January 1952 he was released, as it was against the rules of the institution to treat a patient against his will. The experience embittered Manto toward his family. He started binge drinking, a phase that continued until August 1953, when he had to be hospitalized for cirrhosis of the liver.[45]

Manto's saving grace was his inability to write under the influence. Barring a dozen of his lesser stories and essays, the rest were written while he was stone-cold sober. Typically, he would settle down in the large one-seat sofa at 31 Lakshmi Mansions around two in the afternoon and would not put the pen down until the story or essay he was writing that day had been completed. Nothing distracted him, not the sound of vendors selling their wares outside his doorstep or the noise of children playing. Occasionally he would take time out to resolve outstanding disputes between the children and suggest ingenious ways to make their games more fun and interesting. When he had finished writing, he would go to great lengths to indulge his own children as well as the nephews and nieces living with him. Despite speaking Punjabi at home, Manto communicated with them in Urdu. He did so ostensibly in the interest of promoting a common national language for the new state but actually at the insistence of his elder sister, Iqbal, who after her husband's death had moved with her daughter, Farida, into the top floor of their home at Lakshmi Mansions. He also avoided drinking on national holidays like Pakistan Day on 23 March, not for any nationalist reasons but merely to devote himself to the amusement of the children, whom he helped put up buntings and flags all over the front of the house.[46]

22

Manto with daughters, Nighat and Nusrat, and
niece Sabiha, by Khatir Ghaznavi, Lahore, 1954.
Courtesy Pakistan Academy of Letters,
Government of Pakistan, Islamabad

The vision of Manto celebrating Pakistan Day to inculcate
a sense of national identity among children may seem incon-
gruous with his image as a conscientious objector unrecon-
ciled to partition. Eyebrows might also be raised among those
suspicious of his disdain for the progressive writers, some of
whom are considered to be among the greatest proponents of

good relations between the two hostile subcontinental neighbors. A typical Mantoesque response would be to say that the problem lay with those expressing skepticism—insisting facile consistency implied delusion or dogmatism. He may have doubted the logic of partition, but was the first to raise questions about the kind of films and literature Pakistan needed as an independent Muslim nation-state. With the mullahs raving about their own pet versions of the sharia, the future of art in Pakistan looked bleak. The state had yet to give a lead on the kind of culture envisaged for the Muslim state. Film-makers were wondering whether to build studios, and, if so, how to prevent them from destruction in a war between the two dominions. Some were undecided whether they wanted to live in Pakistan or in India. Those who wanted to market their films in both countries were unsure whether they should portray Hindu characters or only Muslim ones. Would a scene showing an actress reading the Quran and praying enhance or undermine the Islamic character of a Pakistani film?[47]

These questions bore more heavily on matters of national identity than did celebrating either Pakistan Day or Independence Day with children. Manto lost no time taking up cudgels against those seeking to reshape Pakistani society according to Islamic principles. At his satirical best, he wrote about the establishment of a privated unlimited company geared to helping Pakistani women and men who were disinclined to observe Islamic norms of modesty. Women reluctant to don the veil were given a range of options to meet the religious standard in keeping with their class backgrounds. For high-society women, the company had invented burqas made out of glass so that fashionable clothing was perfectly visible. Other types included an air-conditioned burqa cut out of glass cloth for the stiflingly hot summer months; one that spread perfume all around; and one that lit up the entire body in the dead of night. Advance orders of ten thousand of these upper-class burqas had been placed. Middle-class women could purchase burqas that made them visible and invisible at the touch of a button. If they saw a relative approaching, a touch of the button was all they needed to become invisible. Another burqa made middle-class women unrecognizable and was expected to be a sellout. Ironclad burqas would be provided at no cost to poor women; their men could feel completely at ease, since these garments came with locks that could be opened only with numbered keys exclusively issued by the company. Clean-shaven westernized Pakistani men from the upper strata could purchase water-resistant, trouble-free beards and moustaches of all shapes, sizes, and colors to wear whenever they needed to give public speeches or pray in mosques. Special salons were being opened to train middle-class men how to grow beards and moustaches. Those needing a reprieve from the tyranny of hairy faces could hide in a special retreat for up to a month. Special experts were to help men from the poorest strata grow a foot-long beard, thick or thin, within just fifteen days. Machines were being imported from the United States to shave a thousand heads and clip ten thousand upper lips in a single minute.[48]

While Manto could send his readers into stitches on the most serious of issues, he also had a knack for turning the saddest of occasions into moments of renewal and contemplation. In a relatively unknown essay entitled "Hamara Jhanda" (Our Flag), written a few days after Mohammad Ali Jinnah's death, Manto wrote that he had heard a mendicant dervish, passing by on the road, say, "This is not the time to lower the national flag, this is the moment to raise the flag." There was a deathlike silence everywhere. People were weeping. Jinnah was dead. The entire nation, including hundreds of thousands of refugees, felt like orphans. Yet everyone was at work, and suddenly Manto was struck with an epiphany. Mourning for forty days was pointless. The nation had to forge ahead. This was not the time to lower the national flag. Jinnah was not the national flag but the leader who had raised it: "Our flag is Pakistan. . . . not even Pakistan, because that is too limited. Our flag is 'Islam,' whose other meaning is truth. 'This is not the time to lower the national flag, this is the moment to raise the flag.' "[49]

In another equally significant historical intervention Manto queried the curious attitude of the state authorities after the tragic assassination of Pakistan's first prime minister, Liaquat Ali Khan, on 16 October 1951. The murder of the country's most important politician amidst high security in broad daylight was a mystery that required an explanation. Other than revealing the identity of the assassin, the authorities had told the people nothing. Manto thought it incredible that the police had killed the assassin instantly. Two people had been killed, and it was imperative to identify the murderers of both so that those responsible for the crime that had dealt such a bitter blow to the fledgling country could be identified and convicted.[50] What makes Manto such an enthralling witness to history far beyond the moment of partition was his capacity to capture the mood of the wider populace with a few flourishes of the pen. Appreciating his efforts to represent the people's emotions in wanting to see the conspiracy behind Liaquat's assassination flushed out into the open, one enthused reader stated that he had always thought of Manto as a short story writer but now had to change his opinion.

Manto was also a realistic writer who based his work on hard evidence.[51]

Manto's personal struggles and setbacks in Pakistan gave him a perspective on the uneasy nexus emerging between state and society, making him a particularly discerning spectator and critic of the postcolonial moment. "You know me as a short story writer; the courts know me as the writer of obscenity. The government sometimes calls me a communist and, at other times, one of the country's greatest writers. Sometimes the doors to livelihood are closed on me . . . at others they are opened. Occasionally I am declared an unnecessary person and ordered to vacate my home; sometimes out of pleasure I am told I can stay in my home. I used to think and still think about who I am in this country, which is called the world's largest Islamic country. I wonder what is my standing here, what is my purpose." "You may call this is a fictional story," Manto winced, "but for me it is a bitter reality that I have still not found my place in this country called Pakistan, which is very dear to me."[52]

His spirit was restless. At times he was in the antialcoholic ward of Lahore's mental asylum and at others in a hospital. "Whatever I may be, I am sure that I am a human being," he bellowed, with both good and bad qualities. He spoke the truth and occasionally told lies. He did not pray but prostrated himself many times. Nothing saddened him more than people's insensitivity and cruelty toward fellow beings. Insofar as these inhumane traits were attributed to a lack of education, he failed to understand why education was not made universal. Was this not evidence of the fact that those who had control of people's education were themselves uneducated? He just could not fathom what was going on in Pakistan. There was so much inequity and imbalance between the privileged and the dispossessed that he often felt that the relationship between the rulers and the ruled was akin to that between an estranged husband and wife. Then perhaps he was wrong and something very profound was taking place. How could a short story writer grasp why a military agreement was being struck with the United States? A fiction writer could not write an analysis of Pakistan's military deal with Turkey or inquire what had happened to the investigation of Liaquat Ali Khan's murder. But he could ask why there were two enormous holes on the road leading up to McLeod Road without any sign to warn people, and into which he, the great writer of Pakistan, had narrowly escaped falling. If he had died, there would have been a few teary-eyed friends and relatives, but there would be no tears in the country whose asset he considered himself.[53]

For once Manto was wrong. The credit for that goes to his prolific pen, together with the self-belief and hope he never lost despite a string of disappointments and deteriorating health. He may have been happier in Bombay, but it was in Lahore that he wrote some of his finest short stories, as well as personality sketches and essays covering a wide range of subjects. Beginning with "Thanda Gosht" and "Khol Du," he stormed the literary circles with "Toba Tek Singh," which he wrote in 1954 after spending time in Lahore's mental asylum for his alcoholism. Regarded as his best partition story, "Toba Tek Singh" is a scathing comment on the absurdity of the division and the policy of the two postcolonial states to

23
Manto in a pensive mood,
Lahore, no date

split up the inmates of the asylum according to their religious affiliation. Manto's message is searing but clear: the madness of partition was greater than the insanity of all the inmates put together. But beyond partition there were other no less farcical turns in the postcolonial moment that his roving eye, fearless mind, and vibrant pen could not avoid detecting and exposing to the fullest.

Pakistan and Uncle Sam's Cold War

An acerbic critic of progressive follies and the statist fatuities of both subcontinental nations, Manto reserved some of his finest barbs for their respective international patrons—the Soviet Union and the United States of America. He ridiculed the two superpowers for wanting to outdo each other in their quest for world dominance, even if it meant riding roughshod over other countries in the process. His humorous piece "Imaan-o-Iqaan" (Peace and Certainty), written in the form of radio announcements and included in the anthology *Talkh, Tursh aur Shireen* (Bitter, Acrimonious, and Sweet), opens with the United Nations announcing the resolution of the dispute between the superpowers from its headquarters at Lake Success. Instead of persisting with the Cold War, the two rivals have agreed to enter into a contest to prove their military superiority. After duly swearing an oath on uranium and plutonium, each side opts to send a nuclear bomb from its arsenal across to the other's territory so that its lethal potential can be gauged directly. With the UN Security Council in continuous session during the crisis, and much to-ing and fro-ing of the weapons in the air, along with clashing radio broadcasts, the Americans and the Soviets decide to redirect the bombs to some other part of the world. The doomed region where the bombs are headed is none other than the now-divided subcontinent. Both the Indian and Pakistani governments are at their wits' end to decide what to do about the "burning stars" descending on them from the sky. While enlisting the services of their respective clerics for elaborate prayers and entreaties to the heavens, both governments also make extensive arrangements for digging underground cellars and trenches in case the balls of fire come too close for comfort. The piece concludes with Radio Seventh Heaven acknowledging the prayers from the two earthly domains but questioning the faith of the supplicants, who, while lifting one hand solemnly toward heaven, are using the other to dig deep holes and tunnels into the earth.[54]

A humanist and a pacifist who deplored religious hypocrisy with a passion, Manto had come a long way from the days when he imagined driving the British out of India with homemade bombs. He questioned the ethics of possessing weapons of mass destruction—indeed, of militarization itself—when the lives of millions were precarious owing to the lack of access to food, potable water, and other basic amenities of life. He could not stop asking questions. As the elders used to say, questions that arose in the mind could find answers there. This was not true of the question of hunger. It was futile telling starving people about likely improvements in food availability sometime in the future and the heavenly delights awaiting them after death. Hunger required an immediate solution. Insofar as all accepted this as an incontrovertible fact, Manto failed to understand why, instead of bread, the stick was being used to tackle the problem of hunger.[55] Times were strange and newly independent Pakistan stranger still. The gap between the rulers and the ruled was growing by leaps and bounds, making for a disconcerting rift between stated national objectives and actual accomplishments. Except for the graffitied walls, where a surreal freedom of expression was very much in evidence, Pakistan's careworn and gagged citizenry was reduced to watching from the margins the machinations of those in the corridors of power.[56] Unable to partake of the plunder that came in the wake of partition or qualify for allotments of properties, the poor and unconnected could not even begin to hope for government employment, owing to the outright nepotism that Manto exposed in his witty essay "Zaroorat Hae" (Wanted).[57]

Charged with obscenity by the postcolonial government and debarred by the "progressive writers" from publishing in their journals, Manto could not be silenced as long as he knew how to wield the pen to feed himself and his family. Always on the lookout for curious and interesting happenings, he never lacked for subjects to write on. During the height of the Cold War, when the Americans were considering harnessing the Pakistani military in pursuit of their policy to contain the spread of communism, Manto had the brainwave of writing a series of fictitious letters to Uncle Sam, posing as his Pakistani nephew. He could see that the proposed alliance ran against the grain of anti-imperialist sentiments in Pakistan. Displaying a knowledge of international affairs beyond what might be expected of a self-avowedly apolitical writer of fiction, Manto questioned the wisdom of associating Pakistan with an Anglo-American bloc widely accused of perfidy in Palestine and increasingly also in Iran and Egypt. At his perspicacious best, he anticipated the likely consequences of the US-Pakistan alliance for the newly independent country, and many of his predictions have turned out to be correct. First published in 1954 as part of a collection of Manto's humorous essays called *Upar, Nichay aur Darmayan* (Above, Below, and in Between), the letters are an incisive comment on the peculiarities of his adopted country and the fantastical nature of American culture as gleaned from US literature, newspapers, and magazines, and from Hollywood movies. Together with his satirical essays written in the early 1950s, Manto's letters to Uncle Sam offer insights into the Cold War era through the refracting prism of Pakistani politics and society.

Manto wrote the first of the nine letters to Uncle Sam on 16 December 1951, eleven days before being readmitted to the antialcoholic ward of the mental hospital. Of the remaining eight, the second is undated, six were written in 1954, and one went missing in the mail! Manto took the liberty of writing to his esteemed uncle because "you know why my country was carved out of India and how it gained independence." Just as "my country was divided to get independence, I too became independent by being split up." He was born in India, where his mother, father, and firstborn were buried. India was no longer his country; it was Pakistan, which he had seen only five or six times during the period of British subjugation. "Uncle, an all-knowing sage like you would understand what kind of freedom a bird with clipped wings can enjoy." Previously, as India's great short story writer, he was booked for obscenity three times; now, as Pakistan's best short story writer, he had been tried once. But then Pakistan was still young and its government shared the British view of him as a pornographic writer. Actually he was just a poverty-stricken writer who—at the age of thirty-nine, and with twenty-two books to his name—had no house or car of his own. He was poorly paid and had to drink the awful locally distilled whiskey. "If this whiskey were made in your country, you would demolish the distillery with an atom bomb because anyone drinking this dreadful stuff ends up in the netherworld in less than a year."[58]

How he wished Pakistan had courts like those of the United States, the land of seven freedoms, where Erskine Caldwell had been acquitted of obscenity charges for his novel *God's Little Acre*. Manto had been extremely surprised to hear of the case against Caldwell. After all, "you are the king of nudity," and "I thought chastity was called obscenity in your country." If not for the enlightened court judgment, he would have drunk himself to death by consuming large quantities of the local whiskey. It was Pakistan's misfortune to have missed an opportunity to get rid of him. In a play on his first name, which literally means "dutiful," Manto claimed that he was obedient by nature. "I love my country and, by the grace of God, will die in a few days, and if I don't kill myself I will die anyway because where wheat sells at such an exorbitant rate, only a disgraceful person would want to complete his ordained time on earth." He shared the poverty of his compatriots, though not their ignorance. Americans needed to search their own hearts, unless those hearts had been excised by one of their brilliant surgeons, to find out why Pakistan was so poverty-stricken when it had an abundance of imported Packards, Buicks, and Max Factor cosmetics. But then those who drove such cars and used fancy American cosmetics were not of the country. Pakistan was a country of poor people like the author and those who were poorer still. Manto had read Evelyn Waugh's *The Loved One* and was enthralled to learn that in

I know who I am, I will not shun death." His life was like a wall whose plaster he scratched with his nails. Sometimes he wanted to write on all the bricks, and at other moments considered breaking down the wall and rebuilding it anew. Owing to incessant work and his inner intensity, Manto's temperature was one degree above normal. He had much to say and wanted to write a great deal. If only he could get some peace of mind, he might be able to collect his thoughts, which were flying in the air like kites during the monsoons. If someone promised to condense all that was in his mind in a bottle, he was prepared to die instantly. "Manto is alive for Manto," he exclaimed, but of what concern is this to anyone? After all, "what kind of devil is Manto?"[61]

The question assumed added significance in Pakistan, the land of the pure, where the scales were heavily tilted against someone of Manto's disposition and independence of mind. He managed to survive eviction notices issued to him by a government whose left hand did not know what its right hand was doing. His failing health and mounting despondency about the meagerness of his finances subtly reflected the broader social and political malaise that came to grip Pakistan after Liaquat Ali Khan's assassination. Manto was booked on obscenity charges for a second time by the postcolonial state for his story "Upar, Nichay aur Darmayan" (Above, Below, and in Between), with the added inconvenience of having to travel to Karachi for the court hearing in very precarious health. An amusing take on the repressed sexuality of Pakistani upper-class society, the story centers on a sexually revealing exchange between a husband and a wife worried about their son's reading D. H. Lawrence's *Lady Chatterley's Lover*. There was no uproar when the story was first published on 3

February 1952 in the Lahore-based paper *Ehsan*. The problem started when it was reprinted by Karachi's *Qiyam-i-Mashriq* without Manto's permission. A warrant for his arrest was issued in Karachi, but he remained free on bail. The judge turned out to be an admirer and Manto ended up paying a nominal fine of twenty-five rupees after admitting his guilt to save time.

If his ordeal by fire in the postcolonial period on charges of obscenity is a grim reminder of the suffocating persistence of colonial laws, Manto's acquittals confirm the continuing liberal predilections of the Pakistani intelligentsia. But contestations for power and privilege between so-called ideologues of Islam, representing an array of divergent schools of thought, and an equally divided liberal intellectual establishment had already assumed an ugly turn. In the spring of 1953 the heterodox Ahmadi sect had been viciously targeted for political reasons on the grounds that they do not subscribe to the finality of the Prophet Muhammad. There was widespread violence in which several Ahmadis perished before the state intervened to restore order. It was a clear indication of what was in the offing. A weather vane of societal trends, Manto foresaw that attitudes in Pakistan were about to change in significant ways following the signing of the military pact with the United States. This is what seems to have impelled him to write the remaining letters to his uncle. He did not miss the opportunity to rail against his progressive friends in the process of demolishing Washington's conservative allies among the religious right.

The immediate context for the correspondence, as he explains in the undated second letter, was a visit by an official of the US consulate in Lahore who asked Manto to write a short story for an Urdu journal the Americans were bringing out locally. Asked how much he charged for a story, Manto lied and said 200 rupees when he could get 50 at best. The official offered him 500 rupees, which he declined, and so they settled for 300 instead. Manto took the money, making it clear that no changes could be made to what he wrote, which would almost certainly not be to the American's liking. This was the last Manto saw of the official.[62] What followed from his fiendish pen were a set of hilarious asides, and some direct hits too, at America's swelling hubris in the quest for global hegemony during the Cold War. He marveled at the lifestyles of American soldiers who had enough money to feed not one but two bellies. "Our soldiers here don't even make enough to buy half the food they need." "Where do you get all that money from?" he asked impudently, suspecting "fraud" and realizing that his uncle was a "show-off." He wondered why so many Americans wore glasses. "Maybe, it is part of some grand strategy of yours," as the upholders of the "five freedoms," that "you want those whom you can easily put to eternal sleep" to "look at your world through your glasses." Realizing he was crossing a red line, Manto adopted a conciliatory tone. "As long as Pakistan needs wheat, I cannot be impertinent to you." He prayed to God "as a Pakistani (though my government does not consider me a law-abiding citizen)" that if he was alive and Americans ever needed millet, mustard greens, and spinach—the Punjabi staples—he would send them. If his uncle was displeased, he offered to return the 300 rupees, which was already spent, at the rate of one rupee a month.[63]

In March 1954 Manto wrote the third letter after an extended interval, since he had fallen ill after drinking the "blasted" local liquor, which was "poison, pure and simple."

Flaunting his egoism, but also poking fun at his weakness for the toxic alcohol that was killing him, Manto proclaimed himself to be unique. Uncle Sam could not find one like him even with the light of an atom bomb detonation. All he demanded in return was "an announcement" that "your country (may God protect it until the end of the world) will only help my country (may the scourge of God obliterate its distilleries) acquire arms if Saadat Hasan Manto is sent over to you." His value in Pakistan would shoot up at once. He requested that a typical American grin be mailed to him so that he could glue it onto his face to greet the influential people who would undoubtedly flock to his humble home.[64]

Manto liked the American way of life. Though he longed for all things American, he wanted to live in Pakistan, "because I love this bit of earth" whose dust had taken a permanent hold of his lungs. His wish list of American consumer goods included a casual-wear shirt he had seen on an attractive billboard and a Packard. He imagined driving down Mall Road in his new car, wearing the shirt and with a pipe gifted by Uncle Sam stuck between his teeth. On seeing him in such fine fettle, all the progressive and nonprogressive writers of Lahore would realize that they had been wasting their time. Since he needed his uncle to pay for the car's fuel, the nephew promised to write a story entitled "Iran's Nine Maunds [a unit of weight] of Oil and Radha" that would solve the trouble over Iranian oil. More than anything else, he wanted "a tiny, teeny-weenie atom bomb," and for a good cause. The Americans had been doing many such good deeds. "You decimated Hiroshima, you turned Nagasaki into smoke and dust and you caused several thousand American children to be born in Japan." All he wanted to do was to hurl the atom bomb at the Pakistani mullahs and their clones for offending his sensibilities with their coarse notions of hygiene and public propriety. Manto thought the idea of signing a military pact with Pakistan was a tour de force. "You ought to sign one with India as well," and sell both countries discarded Second World War weapons, so that "your armaments factories are no longer idle."[65]

"Let India make all the fuss it wants to, you must sign a military pact with Pakistan because you are very worried about the stability of the world's largest Islamic state. And why not, given that our mullah is the best antidote to Russian communism. Once military aid starts flowing, the first people you should arm are these mullahs. You must also send them American-made rosaries and prayer mats. . . . Cutthroat razors and scissors should be top of the list." The military aid was clearly not for the betterment of the poor; its "only purpose" was to "arm the mullahs" from whose ranks the future clerks and peons would be recruited. Once the mullahs, with their hair trimmed by American scissors and their pajamas stitched by American machines in strict conformity with the sharia, sat on their American-made prayer rugs, the Soviets would have to suspend their activities in Pakistan.[66] In the following letter, the nephew expressed unhappiness with his "respected uncle" for not sending his gift, the atom bomb; he had only wanted "a tiny one." He had also heard that the United States had made a hydrogen bomb so there could be lasting peace in the world. Manto had complete faith in his American uncle but wondered "how many countries will need to be removed from the face of the earth" for "this lasting peace to be established." His niece Farida had asked him to draw a map of the world for her. He had promised to do so after consulting his uncle to "find out the names of the countries that were going to survive."[67]

"I beg you to rid the earth of Russia to begin with because I have a natural aversion to it," the nephew declared. The warm reception his compatriots had recently given to a Russian troupe worried him no end. America urgently needed to send a group of dancers and singers as "a get-even measure"; otherwise, there was a real danger of communism's spreading in Pakistan. He had been urging his uncle to send a "few million-dollar-legged girls from Hollywood" to Pakistan, "but you paid no attention to your foolish nephew and remained preoccupied with your hydrogen bomb experiments." Now the ruling Muslim League had been routed in East Pakistan, and there was every possibility of communism's gaining ground in a country where millions of people could not afford to house, feed, or clothe themselves. Given his poor finances and mounting debts, he too might be coaxed by his communist creditor-friends to leave the comforting shade of the star-spangled banner for the hammer and sickle. Personally the switch would make no difference to him, but people "may cast aspersions on you" and "ask how your nephew got sucked into that nonsense." The only way now to repair the damage was to send Elizabeth Taylor with the troupe and specially instruct her to "kiss me and no one else." Encouraged by the prospect, the nephew was prepared to overlook the new US strategy of "paying greater attention to India." He understood that his good uncle wanted both Pakistan and India to be free from the noxious ideology of communism. Pakistan had to remain free because "you love the Khyber Pass," which had been the gateway for invasions of the subcontinent over the centuries. After all, "what else has Pakistan got!" The Americans were

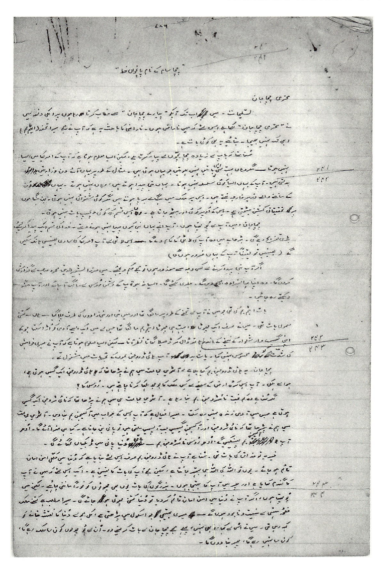

24

Manto's fifth letter

to Uncle Sam

justifiably afraid of the Red Empire's striking roots in India with its hammer and sickle. "I can see that it sends shivers down your spine" to think of India's losing its freedom, which would be a great tragedy considering what Russia had done to Poland, Czechoslovakia, and Korea.[68]

Neither American largesse nor the most artful propaganda was likely to dampen enthusiasm for communist ideas of equality so long as India and Pakistan continued to privilege the interests of the rich over the poor. Making a living in Pakistan was dispiriting, to say the least. "Life here is desolate, bare and harsh," the nephew rued. "I am passing through such bad times that I have forgotten how to pray for good times." It was difficult just to clothe oneself properly. The price of cloth was so exorbitant that the poor could not afford a shroud for burial, while those alive were in tatters. He had decided to open a nudist club. The only problem was that he had no idea what the members could eat—except one another's nakedness, he supposed, but that was hardly an appetizing thought. So he proposed that his venerable uncle seek recourse in soft power rather than single-mindedly pursuing a military alliance with Pakistan. "We will live through our hardships" if "[you] quickly send that goodwill delegation of sweet-voiced, pretty girls," he wrote, adding that "an imprint of Miss Taylor's lips will be most welcome."[69]

Manto's letters skillfully weighed the benefits of US military and economic aid to Pakistan with the concrete gains that could accrue from the extension of American cultural influence. Most Pakistanis were ambivalent, if not opposed, to the proposed alliance. Even a simpleton could tell that the main purpose of American military aid was not the betterment of the common people. The promised economic aid was nothing compared to what India was getting, despite its policy of nonalignment, and would merely end up fattening the bank accounts of the corrupt and already-prospering sections of the ruling elite. This was why the local communists were up to their tricks. Communism was spreading rapidly in the country. In the face of the indifference his uncle was showing toward him, even Manto was thinking of going red. One of his few remaining communist friends, Ahmad Rahi, whom he suspected of filching the sixth letter for party purposes, used to tell him "quite blatantly that whether I admit it or not, I too am a communist." This was just "red mischief." He was as disdainful as ever of the communists and deplored their ungodly ideas and hollow cries of revolution, social equality, and justice.[70] Manto had firmly rejected Rahi's outrageous suggestion that he suspend correspondence with his Uncle Sam and instead start one with Uncle Malenko (the Soviet premier).[71]

If they really wanted to turn the tables on the local communists who were bending over backwards to please the Kremlin, the Americans were better off deploying their cultural muscle, led by the matchless power of their Hollywood film industry. It was appalling to hear about American moviemakers falling all over Indian actresses. "Have all Pakistani actresses croaked that they should be ignored?" He had also heard that Indian filmmakers were going to get American financial assistance. "Uncle, what is the meaning of this?" he asked. "It seems anyone, just anyone, who comes to call on you gets what he wants." "I suggest that you send two or three of your actresses" to Pakistan, Manto wrote, "because our lone hero, Santosh Kumar, is lonely. Recently he went to Karachi, where he drank a thousand bottles of Coca Cola and dreamed of Rita Hayworth all night."[72]

None of this was to deny the inherently Islamic character of Pakistani society. "We Pakistanis are always prepared to lay down our lives for Islam." Earlier Muslims in the subcontinent were ardent fans of both Mustafa Kamal Pasha and Anwar Pasha in Turkey, oblivious of the differences between the two men. Indian Muslims may as well not have existed for the Turks. Unaware of Turkish indifference, "we just loved them, thinking they were our Islamic brothers." Pakistanis were such "simpletons" that they "even loved a certain scented hair oil" simply because it was advertised as "prepared by Islamic brothers." Rubbing the oil in their scalps made Pakistanis feel as if they were in "seventh heaven, compared to which the pleasures of paradise pale into insignificance." When it came to Islam, Manto was only too pleased to instruct his uncle on its blessings, the greatest of which was the provision for men to marry four wives. "In my humble opinion, you should immediately declare Islam as your state religion." Many benefits would accrue from this. With every male citizen taking four wives, the contest between virility and fertility would result in an exponential increase in the American population. "Just think of the difference these numbers would make at the time of war." If Islam were declared the state religion of the United States, there would be no need to conquer Japan and produce illegitimate children. "Uncle, surely you don't condone bastardly acts?" How could one not praise Islam, which offered a simple way out: "Get married and happily procreate."[73]

Manto's bantering tone should not detract from the underlying seriousness of his message. He may not have been an exemplary Muslim, but he knew when his American uncle's drive for influence was beginning to offend the sensibilities of his coreligionists. Similarly, as a staunch Kashmiri, he found it odd that Pakistan and India were fighting over Kashmir and the United Nations was trying to mediate. "Pandit Jawaharlal Nehru is a Kashmiri [like me] and loves Kashmir as I do . . . as any other Kashmiri does." If the great Kashmiri poet Mahjoor were alive, Manto was sure there would be no need for UN negotiators like Dr. Graham (UN mediator Franklin P. Graham).[74] In one of his letters to Uncle Sam he had the audacity to suggest that Washington present a gun to Pandit Jawaharlal Nehru, who was a Kashmiri. It should be a gun that, in keeping with the proverb about Kashmiri unwillingness to fight, would go off on its own when placed in the sun. "I too am a Kashmiri, but Muslim, which is why I have asked for a tiny atom bomb."[75] Intended by Manto as a deterrent to war, if not a magic wand to induce Nehru to be reasonable on Kashmir, his minute atom bomb symbolized the aim of saving lives, as the conventional arming of Pakistan and India would clearly not. "Why don't you start a war between India and Pakistan?" he had cynically asked his American uncle upon hearing of the US economic downturn following the end of the Korean War. "The gains from the Korean War will be nothing compared with the profits from this one. You have your nephew's word." India and Pakistan both would put in rush orders for American arms, giving a much-needed boost to the US economy and, in the process, putting the subcontinent on the road to perdition.[76]

Manto, in his infinite wisdom, had grasped the centrality of the subcontinent in Uncle Sam's game plan against the Soviet Union. American policies during the Cold War were to leave a lasting footprint on the region. Mindful of future complications, the British expressed serious misgivings about the Americans' enlisting Pakistan in the defense of the Middle East and South Asia. First of all, Indians would be livid and even less cooperative than before. And second, it was unclear how the Pakistani military could be used to secure these areas from the threat of communism. Manto was perceptive enough to sense the unacknowledged rivalry between the two Western allies from what he read of the exchanges between the American secretary of state John Foster Dulles and the British foreign secretary Ernest Bevin. He warned the Americans that "Britain is going to create a lot of trouble for you in the future." It ought to be "wiped off the face of the earth," as this "little island will only bring trouble to the world." The second-best option was to fill in the twenty-mile channel separating Britain from Europe.[77] As the British had feared, the flow of US military aid to Pakistan saw India cleaving more closely to the Soviet Union while retaining a formal stance of nonalignment. Domestically the "special relationship" with America had detrimental effects on Pakistan's incipient democracy. The need to bolster defenses against India in furtherance of the irredentist claim on Kashmir had already given the military high command a strong voice in the affairs of state. Once the alliance with America was in place, and the military had confirmed its dominance, the Kashmir issue became significantly more intractable, increasing the trust deficit between Pakistan and India. Heightening animosity between the two neighbors led even a committed peacenik like Manto to look for a way out of the morass of fruitless recriminations and tensions. He had read in the newspaper that the Japanese were unhappy about America's hydrogen bomb tests in the Marshall Islands, which had led to climate change and a longer-than-usual winter. This surprised him, as Pakistanis loved the winter and would like nothing better than to delay the sizzling heat that was once again around the corner. At his mischievous and enterprising best, the devoted nephew asked his uncle to "lob a hydrogen bomb at India" so that he could be "spared the coming summer, which I hate."[78]

Addressing an immediate irritation through drastic action was a tongue-in-cheek comment on the American way of doing things, not a call for the destruction of India, a country that, despite the drawing of a few random lines on the map, remained intrinsic to Manto's personal history. The illogicality of borders between India and Pakistan was the theme of several of Manto's stories, including the classic "Toba Tek Singh," "Titwal ka Kutta" (The Dog of Titwal), and "Aakhri Salute" (The Last Salute). But it was in his short story "Yazid," evocatively translated as "When the Waters Will Flow Again," that Manto provided the most thought-provoking insight into the real nature of Indo-Pakistan enmity. Set against the backdrop of partition violence that had resulted in the death of protagonist Karimdad's father and his wife's brother, the story questions the absurdity of expecting fairness from an enemy. While his wife wallows in grief for her dead brother, Karimdad adopts a stoical position. He counters the villagers' condemnation of his father's murderers with the statement "We are responsible for whatever has happened to us." When war between India and Pakistan seems imminent, the news spreads that India is about to divert the river to starve the village of water. Villagers liken India's threatened blockade of the river water to the legendary cruelty of the Ummayad caliph Yazid toward the Prophet Muhammad's grandson, Husain, and his small party of followers prior to their massacre at Karbala. Manto's allusion to a universal motif of resistance and martyrdom in Muslim consciousness, albeit one with greater emotive meaning for Shias than for Sunnis, underscores the depths of the grievance felt by the Pakistani villagers.[79] India as a whole and Jawaharlal Nehru in particular are reviled. Upon hearing the village headman abuse India, Karimdad stops him and asserts that nothing can be achieved through vilification. Challenging the rhetoric of Indo-Pakistan hostility, Karimdad asks the village headman how a country considered to be an enemy can be expected to show any kindness. Given the opportunity, Pakistanis too would block the flow of India's food and water. After the exchange Karimdad returns home to find that his pregnant wife has given birth to a son. He is delighted and names the boy Yazid, much to the horror of both the wife and the midwife. When his wife asks him how he can give the child such a name, Karimdad says, "It's just a name; it's not necessary that he too will be the same Yazid . . . that Yazid shut the river water; this one will let the waters flow again."[80]

Manto, in his inimitable way, reminds us that the archetypical villain Yazid not only resides in all of us but, with a measure of empathy, can also help dissolve differences with the other to become the ultimate purveyor of peace. Written a few years after partition, "When the Waters Will Flow Again" embodies a moral message that resonates even more loudly today when the two estranged nuclearized neighbors have to weigh the pros and cons of war and peace, of power and principle, of pride and magnanimity in the face of new and more threatening internal and external challenges. Among the most celebrated observers of partition at the moment of its making, in all its psychologically destabilizing but no less reassuring human dimensions—and identified here as an extraordinarily astute interpreter and critic of the postcolonial moment—Manto also needs recognition as a writer whose work has a relevance beyond not only spatial borders but also temporal limitations. So long as the people of the subcontinent remain shackled to their narrowly defined nationalist paradigms, utterly resistant to thinking outside their comfort zones to acquire what Amartya Sen has referred to as a "transpositional understanding" of their opponent's point of view, Manto's life and work will not lose its relevance in reminding them of the pity that was partition, and the pity that partition continues to be.[81]

"I don't have long to live," Manto had written playfully in his seventh letter to Uncle Sam, dated 14 April 1954, and "you alone are responsible for my brief stay on earth."[82] Less than nine months later he was no more. Manto's self-destruction was aided and abetted by a string of enemy friends who plied him with liquor. To the dismay of his family, he borrowed from all and sundry, humiliating himself in the process and going so far as to hide a bottle of whiskey behind the toilet seat in disregard of his penchant for cleanliness. Acquaintances and friends started avoiding him, afraid that he might ask for money to drink the poison that had reduced him to a bag of bones. The immediate family was at their wit's end as to how to keep him from ending his life prematurely. Tired of daily recriminations about his lack of responsibility toward his wife and three young daughters, Manto voluntarily gave Safia the rights to all his writings, past and present. He could no longer borrow anything from any publisher without her prior approval.[83] For a profligate with an alcohol addiction, this was tantamount to a living death.

Saadat Hasan Manto died at 10:30 a.m. on 18 January 1955 after a stormy life lasting a mere forty-two years, eight months, and four days. He was declared out in Lahore during

25
Manto with nephew
Hamid Jalal,
Lahore, ca. 1949

the morning session of the second Indo-Pakistan cricket test match, being played in Bahawalpur. According to his nephew Hamid Jalal, Manto had wanted to see Hanif Mohammad bat in the third test at Lahore.[84] Unlike that slow and steady compiler of a triple century, Manto had played a gem of an innings with an array of spectacular shots before throwing his wicket away. What he lacked in longevity is more than made up for in the folios he has left behind, pages not just of his short stories, but also plays, sketches, and, from a historian's point of view, his largely ignored essays. He died young because he could not stop drinking. On his deathbed he is said to have asked for a peg of whiskey, a spirit synonymous with death that he had embraced as his mortal enemy.[85] He let his liver disintegrate by drinking an excess of the toxic local brew because it somehow connected him with the trials and tribulations of those whose lives were more wretched than his. The tragedy of Manto's life is in many ways the tragedy of Pakistan, the country he reluctantly made his own, but for whose cultural and intellectual renewal he exerted himself and eventually sacrificed his life. Manto was a great short story writer because he was percipient and honest, all too honest. Prejudice was as alien to him as the social hypocrisy he tirelessly strove to uncover. In the end the fatal mixture of religious bigotry and self-serving duplicity made him want to leave the earth prematurely. In a rare prayer to God, Manto pleaded:

Take him away, Lord, for he runs away from fragrance and chases after filth. He hates the bright sun, preferring dark labyrinths. He has nothing but contempt for modesty but is fascinated by the naked and the shameless. He hates sweetness but will give his life to taste bitter fruit. He will not so much as look at housewives but is in seventh heaven in the company of whores. He will not go near running water but loves to wade through dirt. Where others weep he laughs, and where others laugh he weeps. Faces blackened by evil, he loves to wash with tender care to make visible their real features. He never thinks about You but follows Satan everywhere, the same fallen angel who once disobeyed You.[86]

Manto's defiance has been associated with rebellious personalities in both the Western and the Islamic traditions.

He has been likened to Prometheus, who, as punishment for stealing the fire of the gods, was tied to a cliff where an eagle eternally tore at his liver. He has also been compared with the great freethinking Islamic martyr Mansur al-Hallaj, who was sentenced to death for uttering, "An-al-Haq" (I am Truth).[87] Manto's quest for truths that society was averse to acknowledging made him a martyr for many lost causes, and some good ones too. All too aware of the cutting power of his pen, Manto on, 18 August 1954, wrote his own epitaph while obliging a humble stenographer with an autograph. Starting with his mother's recommended use of the numerals 786, which stand for "I begin in the name of Allah, the compassionate, the merciful," he wrote: "Here lies Saadat Hasan Manto. With him lie buried all the arts and mysteries of short story writing . . . Under tons of earth he lies, wondering who of the two is the greater short story writer: God or he."[88]

The pity of Pakistan is that the epitaph does not appear on Manto's grave in the Miani Sahib cemetery in Lahore where he is buried. His bereaved elder sister persuaded the rest of the family not to risk enraging those posturing as the face of religious orthodoxy in the self-consciously Muslim nation-state. So an alternative epitaph, also authored by him, was chosen that was inspired by a couplet from Ghalib: "This is the grave of Saadat Hasan Manto, who still thinks his name was not the repeated word on the tablet of time." It remains to be seen whether there will be less controversy if the final lines of the epitaph are rephrased to read: "Here lies Manto, who is still wondering whether he is the greater storyteller of the past and retriever of memories than the historian."

"A Nail's Debt": Manto Lives On . . .

In 1946 an astrologer in Bombay had predicted that while Manto would live a long life, he was about to enter a seven-year period of hardship and suffering. Manto was then at the peak of his scriptwriting career. The slump in the film industry caused by India's partition had yet to set in. After he passed away sooner than anyone expected, Hamid Jalal mused whether the astrologer had meant that while "Uncle Manto would have a long life as a literary figure . . . his seven year bad period would come to an end with physical death."[1] Saadat Hasan Manto's death stunned and grieved literary and film circles across the divided subcontinent. Friends and admirers in India regretted that someone of his talent had become a victim of a partition they believed should never have taken place. In Pakistan, where he had felt unappreciated and humiliated, Manto was mourned more than any other Urdu writer since the death of the great poet and philosopher Muhammad Iqbal in 1938.[2]

News of Manto's death spread like wildfire within hours of being broadcast on Radio Pakistan, Lahore—ironically, a station prohibited from airing his dramas. The funeral, scheduled for four in the afternoon, took place half an hour earlier, owing to the nature of his illness. By then a galaxy of people from different walks of life had gathered at 31 Lakshmi Mansions to make for a significant, though not traffic-obstructing, procession down the city's main artery on the Mall, via Fane road, to the Miani Sahib graveyard. As the cultural center of Pakistan, Lahore was home to a large number of writers who filled the teahouses where Manto had exchanged ideas with detractors and admirers alike. It was at the Halqa-i-Arbab-i-Zauq on Mall Road that Manto had read several of his short stories and participated actively in literary discussions. In an indication of the postcolonial state's success in typecasting him as a pornographer, alcoholic, and rebel, and of the effectiveness of the progressive writers' ban on him, none of the city's literary luminaries—except for Ahmad Nadeem Qasimi and Mirza Adeeb—showed up to pay him their last respects. The funeral assemblage, which ran into several hundreds, if not thousands, was marked by an overwhelming presence of younger writers, along with students, teachers, and a strong show of solidarity and appreciation from lines of burqa-clad women suspected of being from the red-light district.[3] Proud of his antiestablishment credentials, Manto would not have wanted it any other way. If he was to survive as a writer beyond his short physical life on earth, it was not the old, self-serving literary guard, and their protectors in conservative circles of the establishment, but the restive younger generation of writers and readers who would keep his work alive.

In an imaginative account of the solemn occasion, the literary critic Mumtaz Hasan described the latent tensions that gripped Manto's funeral service. Since Manto did not belong to any literary faction, there were apprehensions that a sectarian brawl might erupt over possession of his body. By the time the troublemakers arrived, socially vilified characters of varying stripes and colors—languishing in poverty while servicing the whims of the rich—had laid claim to Manto's body. A potential clash between these devotees, a dubious-looking cleric, and a menacing-looking group of Sikhs was narrowly averted. But when, in preparation for the funeral prayers, the cleric pulled off his beard and turban and put them aside on the ground, there was uproar among the socially marginalized elements. Grasping the gravity of the situation, the cleric disclosed that he was the main character of Manto's story "Sahib-i-Karamaat" (A Man of God), the tale of a fraudulent mullah who clothes his carnal desires in the garb of religious piety. The mullah noted that Manto was not opposed to the spirit of religion insofar as it related to human well-being and meritorious deeds. But he plainly detested the pretenses of institutionalized religion. So it was only appropriate for the cleric to take off his false accoutrements before starting the funeral prayer. No sooner had these words been uttered than howls of protest broke out, as the majority congregated on the green outside Manto's residence refused to pray behind a religious charlatan. Calmly pleading his case, the cleric noted that Manto never sought pristine purity in anyone and considered even the most aberrant person capable of good deeds. The truth was that righteousness had the greatest effect on sinners, while bad things tempted those who were otherwise considered to be good. "No personal remarks" was the loud retort. Defending his actions in "Sahib-i-Karamaat," the cleric argued that under Islamic law a divorced woman could not remarry her former husband unless she had contracted marriage with an-

and character. Three years before his death, he undertook to compile a book of his friends' observations about his personality. He believed his readers should know as much about him as possible through the eyes of those who knew him well. Inspired by a couplet from his all-time favorite Urdu poet, Ghalib, Manto named the proposed book "Nakhun ka Karz"— literally, a nail's debt. Ghalib had spoken of the heart's sadness because of the half-unknotted thread that only a set of sharp nails could open. As Manto explained to the poet Hafeez Hoshiarpuri, one of the people he asked to write for the volume, "the unraveling of my personality is a nail's debt I want a few of my friends to pay back as soon as possible." Hoshiarpuri agreed to write something, but failed to understand why Manto needed help disentangling his personality, as there was nothing particularly complicated about him. When the two met again a few days later, Hoshiarpuri recited two couplets. Neither was acceptable to Manto, who left, reiterating that his friend still had to repay the debt he owed him. On the occasion of Manto's death, Hoshiarpuri made brevity the better part of valor and wrote movingly:

> In mourning is the art of storytelling today
> That joyfulness of his has departed
> The story on everyone's tongue is
> That Saadat Hasan has departed.[6]

Manto's abrupt leave-taking left many things undone. "A Nail's Debt" was never published. But there was a profusion of writings about his life and work in the immediate aftermath of his death. Newspapers and journals published editorials appraising his work. Poets composed verses lauding his achievements. Condolence ceremonies were held at educational institutions and literary meetings attended by creative writers, literary scholars, and journalists across the country. Even Manto's strongest critics joined the chorus of praise. Resolutions were passed urging the government to provide support for Manto's unfortunate widow and daughters as part of the state's obligation to look after the welfare of Pakistani writers and artists. This was optimism triumphing over experience. There was no support system for literary personalities in cash-strapped Pakistan. Manto's literary corpus even after his death remained an irritant for the regulators of moral health in the Muslim nation-state. Newspapers reported that the deputy commissioner of rehabilitation had turned down a request from an individual who sought to be allotted Manto's residence at 31 Lakshmi Mansions.[7] There was no basis in fact for this rumored gesture of official magnanimity. What did happen was that Manto's nephew Masud Pervez offered to buy the flat and let Safia continue living in it with her daughters. Since the flat was already allotted in Manto's name, the relevant government authorities did no more than transfer the allotment to his wife's name. Safia received no monetary help from the government; nor did she receive royalties from publishers who made handsome profits with several reprints of Manto's works in Pakistan and India. To bring up, educate, and marry her three young daughters, she had to rely on the extended family and the generosity of her brothers. What she did receive in ample measure was sympathy and support from thousands of Manto's admirers and friends, who sent letters and telegrams of condolence. Revered for being the wife of a literary genius, Safia lived out a modest and low-key existence with her mother and daughters at Lakshmi Mansions until her sudden death after a heart attack in 1977.

Uncertain about his place in postcolonial Pakistan, Manto would have been delighted by the honor and respect shown to Safia publicly after his death. The recognition owed nothing to Pakistani officialdom, which continued to represent Manto as a pornographer and a socially subversive writer whom respectable people could not read in the company of their families. Except at sporadic moments, as in the early 1970s under the elected government of Zulfikar Ali Bhutto's Pakistan People's Party and also more recently, Manto's works remained taboo for the government-controlled media, both radio and, from 1964 onwards, also television. There was no question of including any of Manto's short stories in the state-controlled curriculum, whether in schools or in colleges. Despite a virtual state censorship, Manto's works have been published, discussed, and read widely across the subcontinent and, once translated into other languages, also internationally. The chasm between the lack of state sponsorship, if not outright disapproval of his writings, and the growing ranks of Manto enthusiasts made for a creative tension that has served the cause of Urdu literature better than any formal official endorsement would have allowed. Whether in the drawing rooms of the chattering upper and middle classes, in teahouses, or at the meetings of the literary associations dotting the country, Manto's life and work have remained the subject of lively debate in Pakistan, regardless of the policies of a postcolonial state anxious to project its Islamic credentials, or the attitude of conservative circles eager to make social capital out of their contrived piety.

Intent on shedding light on the psychological fallout of societal corruption and moral degeneracy, Manto retaliated against accusations of obscenity by writing even more provocatively to better illuminate what remained hidden under the

26

Manto lives on, by Khatir Ghaznavi, Lahore, 1954.
Courtesy Pakistan Academy of Letters,
Government of Pakistan, Islamabad

Manto's incredible prescience and ability to put his finger on the reality of difficult concepts like jihad in Islam. A first-person narrative, "Shaheedsaz" is about an out-of-work cocaine dealer from Kathiawar in Gujarat. A bania, or moneylender, by caste, he migrates to Pakistan to avail himself of the opportunities to make easy money. Soon after arriving, he ignites the fracas for allotments of properties abandoned by Hindus and Sikhs. After making a bundle on his first acquisition of residential property, he moves from city to city, making friends in high places and lavishing hospitality and largesse on them to get possession of nice houses. Rolling in cash from his lucrative urban real estate, he feels pangs of conscience for not having done anything virtuous since moving to Pakistan. So he begins exploring various possibilities for philanthropy, only to realize that performing good deeds often entails doing something morally reprehensible. For instance, feeding and clothing the poor requires buying these commodities on the black market. After visiting refugee camps, he realizes that charity is habituating people to idleness. How could such people help Pakistan? He thinks of building a free hospital by overinvoicing the costs, only to realize that saving lives would lead to a population explosion, which would severely deplete the nation's limited resources.[9]

Building mosques is equally imprudent, as it would only serve to heighten discord between rival Muslim sects. He decides to go on a pilgrimage to Mecca but drops the idea after reading that those killed in a stampede during a public rally in the city were "martyrs." He confers with religious scholars, who confirm that those dying in accidents are considered martyrs in Islam. What is the point of dying an ordinary death if people can be martyred? He thinks about the issue deeply.

against non-Muslims is a recent construction that selectively draws upon traditional Islamic sources. In the classical Islamic tradition the internal struggle to overcome negative impulses is considered to be the greater jihad (*jihad al-akbar*), while armed struggle is referred to as the lesser jihad (*jihad al-asghar*). With nonstate actors challenging the authority of Muslim rulers and scholars in the contemporary world, radical Muslim groups, linked in one way or another to Al Qaeda, have turned external jihad against the enemies of Islam into the greater jihad.[11] The ingenious transformation of the classical Islamic conception of jihad and martyrdom by these militant groups is a mirror image of the highly ironic interpretation given to it by the main character in "Shaheedsaz."

Manto's flair for anticipating social, political, and intellectual trends gives his work a timelessness that is awe-inspiring and eerie both at once. If Manto is at his philosophical and uncanny best in "Shaheedsaz," the caustic wit in the *Letters to Uncle Sam* offers a masterful reading of the future from the vantage point of a momentous present. Written on the eve of the military pact between Pakistan and the United States, the letters have an unfailing predictive quality. Starting with Manto's suspicion that the military aid was intended for the mullahs, the epistles to Uncle Sam read like an inventory of historic Pakistani gripes against someone mistakenly viewed as an older member of the family. Manto used his literary license to boldly rip through the false pretenses and improbable expectations informing the American-Pakistani relationship, which has proven quite as erratic and bruising as he always assumed it would be. Largely overlooked when they were first published in 1954, other than by literary aficionados and a select circle of devoted readers, his letters to Uncle Sam are today more salient than ever. The rage of anti-Americanism in Pakistan since the US-led invasion of Afghanistan in the fall of 2001 has sparked renewed interest in Manto's factitious letters written in the heyday of the Cold War era. He may not have foreseen the full extent of the destruction and mayhem caused in Pakistan by America's war in Afghanistan. But the letters do provide glimpses into the web of deceit that Manto feared would unavoidably trammel the relationship between two very unlikely allies, pursuing their own mutually contradictory self-interests.

In his own time America's newfangled interest in Islamic Pakistan rankled all the more because Manto recognized it clearly as one of the consequence of India's partition. Since Jawaharlal Nehru wanted to keep independent India out of the entanglements of the Cold War, America could hope to gain a toehold in the subcontinent only by leaning on the weaker, poorer, and needier of the two neighbors. As a pacifist and a humanist, Manto had grave reservations about the American way of dealing with other countries. Money could buy a range of consumer goods and military hardware, not true friendship. Having seen the effects of American influence in undivided India at the tail end of World War II, he was intuitively opposed to linking Pakistan's fate with a recurrently blundering and callous superpower on the global prowl, ever eager to safeguard its own interests at the expense of others. Implicit in Manto's rant against his adopted uncle's flair for wheeling and dealing were concerns about the corrosive effects American arms and greenbacks would have on Pakistan's rapacious ruling elite, which was showing all the signs of dissociative disorder in relating to the ruled.

More measured in his assessment of the Indian leadership, Manto was nevertheless critical of its lack of generosity toward a much smaller and weaker neighbor. At the same time he was unwilling to take sides in the raging disputes between the two nations. His instinct was to try weaning Pakistanis away from an aversion to all things Indian, as in his classic story "Yazid" (When the Waters Will Flow Again), by teaching them the virtues of empathetic understanding. Only by becoming aware of the compulsions and constraints under which Indians operated could Pakistanis come to terms with the reality of the subcontinent's traumatic division and make the most of the boons that had come their way as a result of partition. Manto's refusal to become an instrument in Pakistani officialdom's propaganda wars with India was characteristic of his independent-mindedness. However, it was also a self-conscious effort on his part not to make partition more pitiable by throwing all pretenses at evenhandedness toward the two countries to the winds. Adopting Pakistan as his home never meant disowning India, a country where he was born and spent some of the happiest years of his life, and where his father, mother, and first child were buried.

Whether the reason was his inherent fair-mindedness or the continuing pull of loyalty to the mother country, Manto carefully avoided inflaming relations between India and Pakistan, despite writing on sensitive topics including partition violence, the Kashmir dispute, and American military aid. He might have had an even larger following than the one he has come to enjoy in postcolonial India if, in addition to Hindi and some unauthorized translations in Bengali, his writings had also been available in other regional languages. The box office success of his story for the film *Mirza Ghalib*, which was released in 1954, stands out as a milestone in Manto's life that could have given him real cause to rejoice if not for the discord and disruption partition brought in its wake. He ignored solicitations from friends in India to return to Bombay and resume his career in the film industry, partly for family reasons but also because of animosities between India and Pakistan. Under the circumstances, Manto's ability to spin his magic in the heart of a loyal readership in India is the more remarkable. Indications are that as Manto's writings become more readily available in the regional vernaculars, his following will grow exponentially. A revival of sorts has been underway in India, where the internationally acclaimed Indian actor Naseeruddin Shah has been exhilarating audiences with his theatrical productions of Manto's work.

Internationally too Manto's oeuvre is increasingly becoming better known. Translations of his work, particularly his partition stories and sketches, are being read with increasing enthusiasm. More and more people are discovering the continuing relevance of Manto's works. With the Internet helping make his writings available to a larger and larger readership, Saadat Hasan Manto is today being read internationally far more than he was in his own lifetime. The trend can only grow, since his themes—whether social duplicity, women's sexual exploitation and prostitution, criminality as a product of external ills, or violence mistakenly attributed to religious passions—have a perennial relevance. It is no exaggeration to say that had Manto lived today, he would have been among the pioneers of a literature reflecting the multifaceted social and political ills of our own troubled and disoriented times. That he lives on after death, beyond the territorial confines of the subcontinent, is a measure of the continuing value of his unflinching belief in the intrinsic goodness of human nature—a constant challenge and reminder to people in different ages that it is never too late to search for and speak nothing but the truth.

If there is a cloud hanging over Manto, it is in Islamic Pakistan, where the gap between fact and fiction has been increasing in direct proportion to the decline of interest in scholarly research and the substitution of ideology for a balanced understanding of history. Referring to Mahmud Ghaznavi, the Turkish slave conqueror of the subcontinent whose name is associated with the destruction of the idols at the Somnath temple, Pakistan's poetic and philosophical visionary Muhammad Iqbal once regretted that there was no idol breaker of that caliber left in the world. Manto's literary iconoclasm, notwithstanding his impartiality toward all religious communities, has led to suggestions that he was the answer to Iqbal's complaint, at least in a metaphorical sense.[12] Whether he comes to be accepted as such by those among whom he chose to live and die after partition is far from certain. On 14 August 2012 the government of Pakistan did announce the posthumous award of Nishan-i-Imtiaz (Order of Excellence), its highest civil award, to Manto. Such acknowledgment will have little bearing on Manto's literary legacy, which is already well established. But it could signify the future course of Pakistan as it struggles to break out of the vicious quagmire created by excessive greed and a shocking apathy in the face of human suffering, despite constant invocations of Islam and Islamic piety. Had he been given the choice, Manto would almost certainly have swapped any official recognition of his work for an end to the unconscionable uses of Islam for strategic and political purposes that have plunged the nuclearized subcontinent into a vortex of instability, threatening violence on a scale that is unimaginably worse than anything seen and recorded at the time of partition.

There cannot be a better centenary commemoration of the man whose work captured the pity of partition so poignantly than a grand initiative for honorable peace in the subcontinent. To satisfy the Mantoesque vision, it will have to be a just peace, sensitive to regional aspirations and conducive to promoting the development of creative energies, individually and collectively. Manto's work at the moment of a great historical rupture and its postcolonial aftermath is an overture to that kind of peace. However, the full value of Manto's cosmopolitan humanism will be realized only when the white chalk with which he wrote on the blackboard to enhance its blackness becomes a catalyst for reassessing nationalist narratives through better empathy with others, stimulating a reevaluation of human ethics on a transnational scale.

Notes

Preface

1. Saadat Hasan Manto's first letter to Uncle Sam, 16 December 1951, in *Manto Rama* (Lahore: Sang-e-Meel, 1990), pp. 356–357. For an English translation, see *Letters to Uncle Sam*, trans. Khalid Hasan (Islamabad: Alhamra Printing, 2001), pp. 15–16.

2. Hamid Jalal, "Uncle Manto," in *Black Milk* (Lahore: Sang-e-Meel, 1997), pp. 20–21.

3. Biographical accounts of Manto in English include Leslie A. Flemming's *Another Lonely Voice: The Life and Works of Saadat Hasan Manto* (Lahore: Vanguard Press, 1978) and Alok Bhalla's *Life and Works of Saadat Hasan Manto* (Shimla: Indian Institute of Advanced Study, 1997).

Prelude

1. Saadat Hasan Manto, "Mahboos Auratain" (Interned Women), in *Manto Numa* (Lahore: Sang-e-Meel, 1991), pp. 434–435.

2. Ibid.

3. Saadat Hasan Manto, "Toba Tek Singh," in *Manto Nama* (Lahore: Sang-e-Meel, 1990), pp. 11–18. For an English translation, see *Kingdom's End and Other Stories*, trans. Khalid Hasan (London: Verso, 1987), pp. 11–18.

4. Cited in Ayesha Jalal, *The Sole Spokesman: Jinnah, the Muslim League and the Demand for Pakistan* (Cambridge: Cambridge University Press, 1985), p. 71.

5. Ibid., p. 121.

6. Ayesha Jalal, *Self and Sovereignty: Individual and Community in South Asian Islam since 1850* (London: Routledge, 2000), chap. 9.

7. See, for instance, Veena Das, *Critical Events: An Anthropological Perspective on Contemporary India* (New York: Oxford University Press, 1997); Urvashi Butalia, *The Other Side of Silence: Voices from the Partition of India* (Durham, NC: Duke University Press, 1998); Ritu Menon and Kamla Bhashin, *Borders and Boundaries: Women in India's Partition* (New Brunswick, NJ: Rutgers University Press, 1998); Suvir Kaul, ed., *The Partitions of Memory: The Afterlife of the Division of India* (Delhi: Permanent Black, 2001); Vazira Fazila-Yacoobali Zamindar, *The Long Partition and the Making of Modern South Asia: Refugees, Boundaries, Histories* (New York: Columbia University Press, 2007); Ian Talbot, *Divided Cities: Partition and Its Aftermath in Lahore and Amritsar, 1947–1957,* (New York: Oxford University Press, 2007); Joya Chatterji, *The Spoils of Partition: Bengal and India, 1947–1967* (Cambridge: Cambridge University Press, 2007); Tarun Saint, *Witnessing Partition: Memory, History, Fiction* (New Delhi: Routledge, 2010); and Neeti Nair, *Changing Homelands: Hindu Politics and the Partition of India* (Cambridge, MA: Harvard University Press, 2011).

I
Stories

1. Saadat Hasan Manto, "Sahai," in *Manto Rama* (Lahore: Sang-e-Meel, 1990), p. 20. For an English translation, see "A Tale of 1947," trans. Khalid Hasan, in *A Wet Afternoon: Stories, Sketches, Reminiscences* (Islamabad: Alhamra, 2001), pp. 285–291.

2. Ibid., p. 27.

3. Manto, "Ram Khalawan," in *Manto Rama*, pp. 36–44. For an English translation, see "Ram Khilavan," trans. Aatish Taseer, in *Manto: Short Stories* (Noida: Random House, 2008), pp. 69–78.

4. Mumtaz Shireen, *Manto: Noori na Nari*, comp. Asif Farkhi, 2nd ed. (Karachi: Scheherazade, n.d.), pp. 150–151.

5. See Abu Saeed Qureshi, *Manto (Swaneh)* (Lahore: Idara-i-Faroogh-i-Urdu, ca. 1955), pp. 144–169.

6. Saadat Hasan Manto, "Manto on Manto," in *Bitter Fruits: The Very Best of Saadat Hasan Manto*, ed. and trans. Khalid Hasan (New Delhi: Penguin, 2008), p. 671.

7. Cited in Ali Sana Bukhari, *Saadat Hasan Manto (Tehqiq)* (Lahore: Manto Academy, 2006), pp. 7–8.

8. Interview with Nasira Iqbal, cited in ibid., pp. 12–13.

9. Qureshi, *Manto (Swaneh)*, pp. 26–27.

10. Ibid., p. 23.

11. Ibid., pp. 24–25.

12. Abu Saeed Quershi, "Rahimdil Dahashaat Pasand," *Naqoosh—Manto Number* 49–50 (Lahore: Idara-i-Faroogh-i-Urdu, 1955), p. 340.

13. Qureshi, *Manto (Swaneh)*, p. 26.

14. Bari Alig, "Chand Hafte Amritsar Mein," in *Saadat Hasan Manto, 1912–1955*, ed. Zia Sajjid (Lahore: Maktaba Social Book Service, n.d.), p. 195.

15. Ibid., pp. 196–198.

16. Ibid., p. 198.

17. Saadat Hasan Manto, "Bari Sahib," in *Manto Numa* (Lahore: Sang-e-Meel, 1991), p. 70. For an English translation, see "Bari Alig: The Armchair Revolutionary," trans. Khalid Hasan, in *A Wet Afternoon*, pp. 456–477.

18. Qureshi, *Manto (Swaneh)*, p. 41.

19. Ibid., p. 33.

20. Manto, "Bari Sahib," in *Manto Numa*, pp. 72 and 91.

21. Manto, "Tamasha," in *Manto Rama*, pp. 662–668.

22. Manto, "Bari Sahib," in *Manto Nama* (Lahore: Sang-e-Meel, 1990), pp. 74–75.

23. Qureshi, *Manto (Swaneh)*, pp. 48–50.

24. Ibid., p. 85.

25. Manto to Iqbal, 20 February 1934, Manto's private papers in Nusrat Jalal's possession. All references to this collection are henceforth referred to as "Manto Papers."

26. Ibid.

27. Qureshi, *Manto (Swaneh)*, pp. 62–63.

28. Leslie A. Flemming, *The Life and Works of Saadat Hassan Manto* (Lahore: Vanguard Books, 1985), p. 7.

29. Qureshi, *Manto (Swaneh)*, p. 67.

30. Manto, "Inqilab Pasand," in *Manto Rama*, pp. 633–644.

31. Manto, "Ek Khat," in *Manto Nama*, p. 242.

32. Qureshi, *Manto (Swaneh)*, p. 72.

33. Saadat Hasan Manto to Ahmad Nadeem Qasimi, February 1937, *Manto ke Khutut, Nadeem Ke Naam*, comp. Ahmad Nadeem Qasimi (Lahore: Pakistan Books and Literary Sounds, 1991), pp. 30–31.

34. For an illuminating historical discussion of urban life in Bombay during this period, including Manto's place in it, see Gyan Prakash, *Mumbai Fables: A History of an Enchanted City* (Princeton, NJ: Princeton University Press, 2011), especially chap. 4.

35. Bibijan to Manto, n.d., Letter no. 1, Manto Papers.

36. Hamid Jalal, "Uncle Manto," in *Black Milk* (Lahore: Sang-e-Meel, 1997), p. 18.

37. Meena Menon, "Chronicle of Communal Riots in Bombay Presidency (1893–1945)," *Economic and Political Weekly* 45, no. 47 (20 November 2010): 68–70.

38. Manto, "Aik Aashik Alood Appeal" (A Tearful Appeal), in *Manto Nama*, pp. 574–577.

39. Bibijan to Manto, n.d., Letter no. 2, Manto Papers.

40. Manto, "Meri Shaadi," in *Manto Rama*, p. 291.

41. Manto to Qasimi, September 1938, *Manto ke Khutut*, p. 51.

42. Manto to Qasimi, November 1938, ibid., p. 56.

43. For Manto's fire-walking feat, see Jalal, "Uncle Manto," in *Black Milk*, p. 14.

44. Saadat Hasan Manto, "Sawan-i-Hayat," in *Nau Adarat Manto*, ed. Mohammad Saeed (Lahore: Idara-i-Faroogh-i-Mutala, 2009), pp. 39–40.

45. Manto, "Mein Kyun Likhta Hoon," in ibid., p. 53.

46. Manto to Qasimi, 10 May 1937, *Manto ke Khutut*, p. 40.

47. Manto to Qasimi, May 1937, ibid., p. 42.

48. Bibijan to Manto, n.d., Letter no. 13, Manto Papers.

49. Manto, "New Constitution," in *Black Milk*, pp. 139–149.

50. The clipping was enclosed in a letter from Qaddus Sebhai to Manto, 3 August 1945, Manto Papers.

51. Manto to Qasimi, January 1940, *Manto ke Khutut*, p. 98.

52. Manto to Qasimi, September 1938, ibid., p. 49.

53. Manto to Qasimi, June 1939, ibid., p. 77.

54. Manto to Qasimi, 23 September 1940, ibid., pp. 135–136, 138.

55. Balwant Singh Gargi, "Haseen Chehray: Saadat Hasan Manto," in *Manto ke Behtareen Afsaaney*, comp. Athar Parvez (Lahore: Shakarganj Printers, n.d.), p. 10.

56. Manto, "Safaid Jhoot," in *Manto Rama*, p. 675.

57. Cited in Sugata Bose and Ayesha Jalal, *Modern South Asia: History, Culture, Political Economy*, 2nd ed. (London: Routledge, 2004), p. 131.

58. Bukhari, *Saadat Hasan Manto (Tehqiq)*, p. 56.

59. Manto to Qasimi, May 1943, *Manto ke Khutut*, p. 175.

60. Gargi, "Haseen Chehray: Saadat Hasan Manto," in *Manto ke Behtareen Afsaaney*, p. 11.

61. Manto, "Mootri," in *Manto Rama*, pp. 162–163. For an English translation, see "Three Simple Statements," trans. Khalid Hasan, in *A Wet Afternoon*, pp. 259–260.

62. Manto, "Thalia the Pimp," in *Black Milk*, pp. 47–56.

63. Manto, "Tayaqqun," in *Manto Rama*, pp. 475–481. For an English translation, see "The Dutiful Daughter," trans. Khalid Hasan, in *A Wet Afternoon*, pp. 254–258.

64. Manto, "Nothing but the Truth," in *Black Milk*, pp. 129–137.

II
Memories

1. Saadat Hasan Manto, "Thalia the Pimp," trans. Hamid Jalal, in *Black Milk* (Lahore: Sang-e-Meel, 1997), p. 48.

2. Urvashi Butalia, "Community, State and Gender: On Women's Agency during Partition," *Economic and Political Weekly*, 24 April 1993, p. 12.

3. Saadat Hasan Manto, "Ganjay Farishtay" (Bald Angels), in *Manto Numa* (Lahore: Sang-e-Meel, 1991), pp. 224, 226.

4. Ibid., p. 230.

5. Manto to Qasimi, May 1937, Ahmad Nadeem Qasimi, *Manto ke Khutut, Nadeem Ke Naam*, comp. Ahmad Nadeem Qasimi (Lahore: Pakistan Books and Literary Sounds, 1991), pp. 41–43.

6. Rajinder Singh Bedi to Manto, 28 August (no year, Lahore), Manto Papers.

7. Bedi to Manto, 11 September 1940 (Lahore), Manto Papers.

8. Bedi to Manto, 30 September 1940 (Lahore), Manto Papers.

9. Krishan Chander, *Naye Adab Ke Maimar—Saadat Hasan Manto* (Bombay: Kutub Publishers, 1948), p. 13.

10. Krishan Chander, "Saadat Hasan Manto," in *Saadat Hasan Manto, 1912–1955*, ed. Zia Sajjid (Lahore: Maktaba Social Book Service, n.d.), p. 13.

11. Krishan Chander to Manto, 20 September 1940 (Delhi), Manto Papers.

12. Krishan Chander to Manto, 17 October 1940 (Delhi), Manto Papers.

13. Letter of introduction by Hamid Ali Khan, joint editor of the *Humayun*, 15 April 1939, Manto Papers.

14. Abu Saeed Qureshi, *Manto (Swaneh)* (Lahore: Idara-i-Faroogh-i-Urdu, ca. 1955), pp. 76–83.

15. Saadat Hasan Manto, "Aao Suno," in *Manto Dramay* (Lahore: Sang-e-Meel, 1996), p. 265.

16. Krishan Chander, "Saadat Hasan Manto', in Sajjid, ed., *Saadat Hasan Manto*, p. 13.

17. Islamic cosmology and mythology consider the Qaf Mountains to be the point where heaven and earth meet. In the Quran, the Qaf Mountains are associated with the seven holy sleepers in the cave.

18. Qureshi, *Manto (Swaneh)*, p. 87.

19. Upendranath Ashk, "Manto—'Mera Dushman,'" *Naqoosh—Manto Number*, 49–50 (Lahore: Idara-i-Faroogh-i-Urdu, 1955), pp. 328–329.

20. Devendra Satyarthi to Manto, 3 April 1941 (Lahore), Manto Papers.

21. Ashk, "Manto—'Mera Dushman,'" *Naqoosh—Manto Number*, p. 312.

22. Ibid.

23. Upendranath Ashk, *Manto: Mera Dushman* (Allahabad: Naya Idarah, 1979).

24. Qureshi, *Manto (Swaneh)*, p. 98.

25. Ashk, "Manto—'Mera Dushman,'" *Naqoosh—Manto Number*, p. 315.

26. Leslie Flemming, "Other Reflections: The Minor Writings of Saadat Hasan Manto," *Journal of South Asian Literature* 20, no. 2, The Writings of Saadat Hasan Manto (Summer, Fall 1985): 134.

27. Chander, *Naye Adab Ke Maimar—Saadat Hasan Manto*, p. 18. Also Krishan Chander to Manto, 28 November 1942 (Lucknow), Manto Papers.

28. Cited in Ali Sana Bukhari, *Saadat Hasan Manto (Tehqiq)* (Lahore: Manto Academy, 2006), p. 191.

29. Ashk, "Manto—'Mera Dushman,'" *Naqoosh—Manto Number*, p. 314.

30. Chander, *Naye Adab Ke Maimar—Saadat Hasan Manto*, p. 18.

31. Ashk, "Manto—'Mera Dushman,'" *Naqoosh—Manto Number*, p. 314.

32. Manto to Qasimi, 1 April 1942, *Manto ke Khutut*, p. 165.

33. Qureshi, *Manto (Swaneh)*, p. 113.

34. Manto, "Journalist," in *Manto Dramay*, pp. 141, 146–147.

35. Manto, "Jaib Katra," in *Manto Dramay*, pp. 92–106.

36. Balwat Singh Gargi, "Haseen Chehray: Saadat Hasan Manto," in *Manto ke Behtareen Afsaaney*, comp. Athar Parvez (Lahore: Sha-karganj Printers, n.d.), pp. 11–12.

37. Manto, "Paish Lafz" (Preface), in *Manto Dramay*, p. 11.

38. Leslie Flemming, *Another Lonely Voice: The Life and Works of Saadat Hassan Manto* (Lahore: Vanguard Books, 1978), p. 11.

39. Manto, "Paish Lafz" (Preface), *Teen Auratain*, in *Manto Dramay*, p. 481.

40. In a rare gesture for a Pakistani publisher, Dehalvi returned the copyright of both books to Safia on the occasion of Manto's death. Qureshi, *Manto (Swaneh)*, pp. 115–118.

41. Saadat Hasan Manto, "Meri Shaadi" (My Wedding), in *Manto Rama* (Lahore: Sang-e-Meel, 1990), p. 284.

42. Qureshi, *Manto (Swaneh)*, p. 114.

43. Manto, "Khalid Mian," in *Manto Rama*, pp. 72–81. For an English translation, see "Khaled Mian," trans. Aatish Taseer, in *Manto: Short Stories* (Noida: Random House, 2008), pp. 33–44.

44. Saadat Hasan Manto, "Lazat-i-Sang" (Taste of Stone), in *Manto Nama* (Lahore: Sang-e-Meel, 1990), pp. 648–649.

45. Ahmad Nadeem Qasimi, "Saadat Hasan Manto," *Naqoosh—Lahore Number*, ed. Mohammad Tufail (Lahore: Idara-i-Faroogh-i-Urdu), no. 92 (February 1962), pt. 2, p. 1098.

46. Manto to Qasimi, July 1942, *Manto ke Khutut*, p. 165.

47. Bukhari, *Saadat Hasan Manto (Tehqiq)*, p. 55.

48. Nazir Ahmad (Hind Pictures) to Manto, 27 July 1942, Manto Papers.

49. Qureshi, *Manto (Swaneh)*, pp. 112–113.

50. Chander, *Naye Ke Maimar—Saadat Hasan Manto*, p. 19.

51. See Ayesha Jalal, *The Sole Spokesman: Jinnah, the Muslim League and the Demand for Pakistan* (Cambridge: Cambridge University Press, 1985), passim.

52. Manto, "Hindustan ko Lidroon say Bachaoo" (Save India from Leaders), in *Manto Numa*, pp. 571–573.

53. See above, pp. 56–58.

54. Manto, "Ismat Chughtai," in *Manto Numa*, pp. 101–102. For an English translation, see "Ismat Chughtai," trans. Mohammad Asaduddin, *Annual of Urdu Studies* 16 (2001): 201–215.

55. Ismat Chughtai, "Mera Dost, Mera Dushman," *Naqoosh— Manto Number*, p. 298. For an English translation, see *My Friend, My Enemy: Essays, Reminiscences, Portraits*, trans. Tahira Naqvi (New Delhi: Kali for Women, 2001), pp. 190–212.

56. Manto, "Ismat Chughtai," in *Manto Numa*, p. 102.

57. http://www.columbia.edu/itc/mealac/pritchett/00urdu/ ismat/txt_ismat_interview_mahfil1972.html#n03.

58. Manto, "Ismat Chughtai," in *Manto Numa*, p. 107.

59. Chughtai, "Mera Dost, Mera Dushman," *Naqoosh—Manto Number*, pp. 296–300.

60. Manto, "Paish Lafz" (Preface), in *Manto Rama*, pp. 699–706. For an English translation, see "Modern Literature," trans. Bilal Tanweer, in *Manto*, ed. Ayesha Jalal and Nusrat Jalal (Lahore: Sang-e-Meel Publications, 2012), pp. 12–18.

61. For Manto's account and self-defense, see "Lazat-i-Sang" (Taste of Stone), in *Manto Nama*, pp. 613–640.

62. Manto, "Ismat Chughtai," in *Manto Numa*, p. 108. For Ismat's account, see Ismat Chughtai, *A Life in Words: Memoirs*, trans. M. Asaduddin (New Delhi: Penguin, 2012), pp. 24–37.

63. Manto, "Ismat Chughtai" and "Pari Chehra Naseem Bano," in *Manto Numa*, pp. 108–109, 153–154. For an English translation of the latter, see "Naseem: The Fairy Queen," trans. Khalid Hasan, in *A Wet Afternoon: Stories, Sketches, Reminiscences* (Islamabad: Al-hamra, 2001), pp. 651–665.

64. Manto, "Batein," in *Manto Rama*, p. 389.

65. Ibid., pp. 390–391.

66. Manto to Qasimi, 1 October 1945, *Manto ke Khutut*, p. 180.

67. Manto to Qasimi, February 1947, ibid., p. 185; Hamid Jalal to Manto, 11 February 1947, Manto Papers. Also Manto, "Ashok Kumar," in *Manto Numa*, pp. 173–174; for an English translation, see "Ashok Kumar: The Evergreen Hero," trans. Khalid Hasan, in *A Wet Afternoon*, pp. 478–494.

68. Bukhari, *Saadat Hasan Manto (Tehqiq)*, pp. 60–61.

69. Hamid Jalal to Manto, 6 February 1947, Manto Papers.

70. Manto, "Ashok Kumar," in *Manto Numa*, p. 174.

71. Ibid., pp. 174–176.

72. Manto, "Inqilab Pasand," in *Manto Rama*, p. 641.

73. For an intriguing take on Manto's critique of mainstream Indian nationalism from a literary perspective, see Amir R. Mufti, *Enlightenment in the Colony: The Jewish Question and the Crisis of Postcolonial Culture* (Princeton, NJ: Princeton University Press, 2007), chap. 4.

74. Manto, "Batein," in *Manto Rama*, p. 392.

75. Manto, "Murli ki Dhun," in *Manto Numa*, pp. 118, 122, 127, 130–131. For an English translation, see "Shyam: Krishna's Flute," trans. Khalid Hasan, in *A Wet Afternoon*, pp. 524–544.

76. Ibid., p. 135.

77. Manto, "Murli ki Dhun," in *Manto Numa*, pp. 136–137.

78. Bukhari, *Saadat Hasan Manto (Tehqiq)*, p. 61.

79. Manto, "Murli ki Dhun," in *Manto Numa*, p. 137.

80. Manto, "Ashok Kumar," in *Manto Numa*, p. 176.

81. Manto, "Murli ki Dhun," in *Manto Numa*, pp. 137–138.

82. Chughtai, "Mera Dost, Mera Dushman," *Naqoosh—Manto Number*, pp. 308–309.

83. Saadat Hasan Manto, *A Wet Afternoon*, trans. Khalid Hasan, pp. 52–57.

84. Manto, "Jaib-i-Kafan," in *Manto Nama*, pp. 221–222.

85. Manto, "Murli ki Dhun," in *Manto Numa*, p. 132.

86. Manto, "Ashok Kumar," in *Manto Numa*, p. 164.

87. Agha Khalash Kashmiri to Manto, 17 November 1952, Manto Papers.

88. Manto, "Murli ki Dhun," in *Manto Numa*, p. 138.

89. Ibid., p. 132.

90. Ibid., pp. 132–135.

91. Amrita Pritam to Manto, 26 June 1954, Manto Papers.

92. Manto, "Murli ki Dhun," in *Manto Numa*, p. 137.

III

Histories

1. Saadat Hasan Manto, "Qatal-o-Khoon ki Lakirain" (Murder and Lines of Blood), in *Manto Rama* (Lahore: Sang-e-Meel, 1990), pp. 302–303.

2. Manto, "Tayaqqun," in *Manto Rama*, p. 476.

3. Ibid., pp. 476–477.

4. Saadat Hasan Manto, "Mahboos Auratain" (Interned Women), in *Manto Numa* (Lahore: Sang-e-Meel, 1991), pp. 434–436.

5. Manto, "Qatal-o-Khoon ki Lakirain" (Murder and Lines of Blood), in *Manto Rama*, pp. 303–305.

6. Ibid., pp. 351–352.

7. Saadat Hasan Manto, "Toba Tek Singh," in *Manto Nama* (Lahore: Sang-e-Meel, 1990), pp. 11–18.

8. Manto, "Zehmat-i-Mehr-i-Darakhshan," in *Manto Nama*, p. 353. For an abridged English translation, see "Manto's Day in Court," trans. Khalid Hasan, in *A Wet Afternoon: Stories, Sketches, Reminiscences* (Islamabad: Alhamra, 2001), pp. 694–703.

9. Ibid., pp. 352–354, and also see below.

10. Manto, "Thanda Gosht," in *Manto Nama*, pp.404–411. For an English translation, see "Colder than Ice," trans. Khalid Hasan, in *A Wet Afternoon*, pp. 52–57.

11. Saadat Hasan Manto, "Khol Du," in *Manto Kahanian* (Lahore: Sang-e-Meel, 1995), pp. 11–14. For an English translation, see "The Return," trans. Khalid Hasan, in *A Wet Afternoon*, pp. 78–81.

12. Manto, "Zehmat-i-Mehr-i-Darakhshan," in *Manto Nama*, p. 355.

13. Ahmad Nadeem Qasimi, "Urdu Afsaneh Mein Haqiqat Pasandi aur Juratmandi ki Misaal, Manto," *Imroze Haftroza Ishaat*, 21 January 1968.

14. Manto, "Zehmat-i-Mehr-i-Darakhshan," in *Manto Nama*, p. 357.

15. Ibid., pp. 357–358.

16. Manto had hired Tassaduq Hussain Khalid as his lawyer. Sheikh Khurshid Ahmad, Mazhar-ul-Haq, Ejaz Ahmad Khan,

and Sardar Mohammad Iqbal were the four attorneys who stepped forward to help him in Khalid's absence. Ali Sana Bukhari, *Saadat Hasan Manto (Tehqiq)* (Lahore: Manto Academy, 2006), pp. 72–73.

17. Manto, "Zehmat-i-Mehr-i-Darakhshan," in *Manto Nama*, pp. 374–378.

18. Ibid., pp. 384–389.

19. Judgment of the Additional Sessions Court Judge (Lahore), Inayatullah Khan, 10 July 1950, Manto Papers.

20. Kausar Anwari to Manto, 9 May 1949 (Lahore), Manto Papers.

21. Mir Tajammul Hussain to Manto, February 1950 (Mysore), Manto Papers.

22. Balwant Singh to Manto, 25 July 1950 (Delhi), Manto Papers.

23. Mahmud Saleem to Manto, 12 July 1950 (Gujranwala), Manto Papers.

24. Khalid to Manto, 7 September 1948 (Lahore), Manto Papers.

25. Sajjad Zaheer, *The Light: A History of the Movement for Progressive Literature in the Indo-Pak Subcontinent*, a translation of *Roshnai* by Amina Azfar (Karachi: Oxford University Press, 2006). Also see Ali Husain Mir and Raza Mir, *Anthems of Resistance* (New Delhi: Roli Books, 2011).

26. Sarah Waheed, "Radical Politics and the Urdu Literary World in the Era of South Asian Nationalisms c. 1919–1952" (PhD diss., Tufts University, December 2010), chap. 3.

27. Muhammad Umar Memon, "Askari's 'Noun' and Tasavvuf" (translator's note), *Annual of Urdu Studies*, no. 19 (2004): 260–272.

28. Leslie Flemming, "Ahmad Nadeem Qasmi: A Friend and Colleague Reminisces," *Journal of South Asian Literature* 20, no. 2, The Writings of Saadat Hasan Manto (Summer, Fall 1985): 147–151.

29. Ali Sardar Jafri to Manto, 7 July 1948 (Bombay), Manto Papers.

30. Ali Sardar Jafri to Manto, 17 August 1948 (Bombay), Manto Papers.

31. Ali Sardar Jafri to Manto, 7 September 1948 (Bombay), Manto Papers.

32. Ali Sardar Jafri to Manto, 23 September 1948 (Bombay), Manto Papers.

33. Ali Sardar Jafri to Manto, 10 December 1948 (Bombay), Manto Papers.

34. Bukhari, *Saadat Hasan Manto (Tehqiq)*, p. 68.

35. Upendranath Ashk to Manto, 28 August 1950 (Allahabad), Manto Papers.

36. Roshan Nagyoni to Manto, 6 August 1950 (Rawalpindi), Manto Papers.

37. Manto, "Paish Lafz" (Preface), in *Manto Rama*, pp. 700–701, 704.

38. Manto, "Deebacha" (Introduction), in *Manto Nama*, pp. 344–347.

39. Manto, "Jaib-i-Kafan" (Shroud's Pocket), in *Manto Nama*, pp. 222–223.

40. Ibid., pp. 224–225.

41. Ibid., pp. 226–228.

42. Mohammad Hasan Askari, "Manto ke Afsaneh," January–February 1951, in *Askarinama: Afsaneh aur Mazameen* (Lahore: Sang-e-Meel, 1998), pp. 419–424.

43. Bukhari, *Saadat Hasan Manto (Tehqiq)*, p. 67.

44. Hamid Jalal, "Uncle Manto," in *Black Milk* (Lahore: Sang-e-Meel, 1997), p. 31.

45. Ibid., p. 27.

46. Ibid., pp. 27–28.

47. Saadat Hasan Manto, "Pakistan ke Film," *Imroze* (Lahore), 15 August 1948, in *Nau Adarat Manto*, ed. Mohammad Saeed (Lahore: Idara-i-Faroogh-i-Mutala, 2009), pp. 105–109.

48. Manto, "Darhi, Mounch, Burqa Unlimited" (Beard, Moustache, Burqa Unlimited), *Imroze* (Lahore), 30 August 1948, in ibid., pp. 110–112. For an English translation, see "Beard, Mustache, Burqa Unlimited," trans. Bilal Tanweer, in *Manto*, ed. Ayesha Jalal and Nusrat Jalal, pp. 155–157.

49. Manto, "Hamara Jhanda" (Our Flag), *Imroze* (Lahore), 14 September 1948, in *Nau Adarat Manto*, ed. Mohammad Saeed, pp. 113–115.

50. Manto, "Qatal, Qatil aur Maqtool aik Frame Mein" (Murder, Murderer and the Murdered in One Frame), *Afaaq* (Lahore), 23 October 1951, in ibid., pp. 116–123. For an English translation, see "Murder, Murderer and the Murdered—In One Shot," trans. Mujahid Eshai, in *Manto*, ed. Ayesha Jalal and Nusrat Jalal, pp. 158–162.

51. Tajuddin Ahmad Taj to Manto, 23 October 1951 (Lahore), Manto Papers.

52. Manto, "Do Garhay" (Two Craters), in *Manto Rama*, p. 408. For an English translation, see "Two Potholes," trans. Bilal Tanweer, in *Manto*, ed. Ayesha Jalal and Nusrat Jalal, pp. 163–169.

53. Ibid., pp. 408–413.

54. Manto, "Imaan-o-Iqaan," in *Manto Numa*, pp. 439–444.

55. Manto, "Sawal Paida Hota Hae" (The Question Arises), in ibid., p. 408.

56. Manto, "Dewaaroon Peh Likhna" (Writing on the Walls), in ibid., pp. 390–391.

57. Manto, "Zaroorat Hae" (Wanted), in *Manto Rama*, pp. 272–275.

58. Manto's first letter to Uncle Sam, 16 December 1951, in *Manto Rama*, pp. 356–357. For an English translation, see *Letters to Uncle Sam*, trans. Khalid Hasan (Islamabad: Alhamra Printing, 2001).

59. Ibid., pp. 360–362.

60. Jalal, *Black Milk*, p. 19.

61. Manto to Qasimi, 12 February 1939, in, *Manto ke Khutut, Nadeem Key Naam*, comp. Ahmad Nadeem Qasimi (Lahore: Pakistan Books and Literary Sounds, 1991), pp. 70–71.

62. Manto's second letter to Uncle Sam, n.d., in *Manto Rama*, pp. 373–374.

63. Ibid. and *Letters to Uncle Sam*, pp. 28–29, 33–35.

64. Manto's third letter to Uncle Sam, 15 March 1954, in *Manto Rama*, pp. 384–385, and *Letters to Uncle Sam*, pp. 38–41.

65. Manto's third letter to Uncle Sam, 15 March 1954, in *Manto Rama*, pp. 386–387, and *Letters to Uncle Sam*, pp. 42–44.

66. Manto's fourth letter to Uncle Sam, 21 February 1954, in *Manto Rama*, pp. 393–394.

67. Manto's fifth letter to Uncle Sam, n.d., in ibid., pp. 402–403, and *Letters to Uncle Sam*, pp. 58–60.

68. Ibid., pp. 403–406, and *Letters to Uncle Sam*, pp. 60, 63–64.

69. Ibid., p. 406, and *Letters to Uncle Sam*, pp. 64–65.

70. Manto's ninth letter to Uncle Sam, 26 April 1954, in *Manto Rama*, p. 443, and *Letters to Uncle Sam*, p. 104.

71. Manto's eighth letter to Uncle Sam, 22 April 1954, in *Manto Rama*, p. 434, and *Letters to Uncle Sam*, p. 86.

72. Manto's fourth letter to Uncle Sam, 21 February 1954, in *Manto Rama*, p. 396, and *Letters to Uncle Sam*, p. 53.

73. Manto's eighth letter to Uncle Sam, 22 April 1954, in *Manto Rama*, p. 436, and *Letters to Uncle Sam*, pp. 88, 90.

74. Manto, "Shair-i-Kashmir—Mahjoor Kashmiri," in Saeed, *Nau Adarat Manto*, pp. 128–130.

75. Manto's third letter to Uncle Sam, 15 March 1954, in *Manto Rama*, pp. 386–387, and *Letters to Uncle Sam*, p. 44.

76. Manto's seventh letter to Uncle Sam, 14 April 1954, in ibid., pp. 419–420, and *Letters to Uncle Sam*, p. 77.

77. Ibid., p. 420, and *Letters to Uncle Sam*, p. 79.

78. Manto's ninth letter to Uncle Sam, 26 April 1954, in *Manto Rama*, p. 447, and *Letters to Uncle Sam*, p. 110.

79. For a broader discussion of the trope of Karbala, see Syed Akbar Hyder, *Reliving Karbala: Martyrdom in South Asian Memory* (New York: Oxford University Press, 2006), especially pp. 197–199.

80. Manto, "Yazid," in *Manto Nama*, pp. 99–108.

81. Amartya Sen, *The Idea of Justice* (London: Penguin Books, 2010), chap. 7.

82. Manto's seventh letter to Uncle Sam, 14 April 1954, in *Manto Rama*, p. 419, and *Letters to Uncle Sam*, pp. 75–76.

83. Jalal, "Uncle Manto," in *Black Milk*, p. 32.

84. Ibid., p. 29.

85. Ibid., p. 34.

86. "Manto's Prayer," trans. Khalid Hasan, in *A Wet Afternoon*, p. 704.

87. Abu Saeed Qureshi, *Manto (Swaneh)* (Lahore: Idara-i-Faroogh-i-Urdu, ca. 1955), p. 48.

88. Ibid., p. 705.

Epilogue

1. Hamid Jalal, *Black Milk* (Lahore: Sang-e-Meel, 1997), pp. 19–20.

2. Mohammad Hasan Askari, "Manto ka Muqam" (Manto's Stature), *Naqoosh—Manto Number*, 49–50 (Lahore: Idara-i-Faroogh-i-Urdu, 1955), p. 250.

3. Intizar Hussain, cited in Ali Sana Bukhari, *Saadat Hasan Manto (Tehqiq)* (Lahore: Manto Academy, 2006), p. 89.

4. Mumtaz Hasan, "Saadat Hasan ki Yaad Mein" (In Saadat Hasan's Memory), *Naqoosh—Manto Number*, pp. 289–290.

5. Ibid., pp. 292–295.

6. Hafeez Hoshiarpuri, "Nakhun Ka Karz" (A Nail's Debt), *Weekly Tameer* (Rawalpindi) 6, no. 124 (31 January 1955).

7. *Imroze* (Lahore), 8 February 1955.

8. Mohammad Hasan Askari, "Manto ka Muqam" (Manto's Station), *Naqoosh—Manto Number*, p. 249.

9. Saadat Hasan Manto, "Shaheedsaz" (Martyr Maker), in *Manto Kahanian* (Lahore: Sang-e-Meel, 1995), pp. 92–98. For an English translation, see "Doing God's Work," trans. Khalid Hasan, in *Bitter Fruits: The Very Best of Saadat Hasan Manto* (New Delhi: Penguin, 2008), pp. 258–263.

10. Ibid.

11. See Ayesha Jalal, *Partisans of Allah: Jihad in South Asia* (Cambridge, MA: Harvard University Press, 2008), chaps. 1 and 5.

12. Abu Saeed Qureshi, *Manto (Swaneh)* (Lahore: Idara-i-Faroogh-i-Urdu, ca. 1955), p. 38.

Select Bibliography

Manto Papers

The collection—consisting of letters, some by Manto but mainly those he received from relatives, friends, and admirers; published and unpublished handwritten manuscripts of his short stories and screenplays; as well as a collection of photographs—is in Nusrat Jalal's possession in Lahore.

English

BOOKS

Bhalla, Alok. *Life and Works of Saadat Hasan Manto*. Shimla: Indian Institute of Advanced Study, 1997.

Chughtai, Ismat. *A Life in Words: Memoirs*. Translated by M. Asaduddin. New Delhi: Penguin, 2012.

Flemming, Leslie A. *Another Lonely Voice: The Life and Works of Saadat Hasan Manto*. Lahore: Vanguard Press, 1978.

Hasan, Khalid, trans. *Bitter Fruits: The Very Best of Saadat Hasan Manto*. New Delhi: Penguin, 2008.

———. *Kingdom's End and Other Stories*. London: Verso, 1987.

Hasan, Khalid. *Letters to Uncle Sam*. Islamabad: Alhamra Printing, 2001.

———. *A Wet Afternoon: Stories, Sketches, Reminiscences*. Islamabad: Alhamra, 2001.

Jalal, Ayesha. *Partisans of Allah: Jihad in South Asia*. Cambridge, MA: Harvard University Press, 2008.

———. *Self and Sovereignty: Individual and Community in South Asian Islam since 1850*. London: Routledge, 2000.

———. *The Sole Spokesman: Jinnah, the Muslim League and the Demand for Pakistan*. Cambridge: Cambridge University Press, 1985.

Jalal, Ayesha, and Nusrat Jalal, eds. *Manto*. Lahore: Sang-e-Meel Publications, 2012.

Jalal, Hamid. *Black Milk*. Lahore: Sang-e-Meel, 1997.

Mir, Ali Husain, and Raza Mir. *Anthems of Resistance*. New Delhi: Roli Books, 2011.

Naqvi, Tahira, trans.. *My Friend, My Enemy: Essays, Reminiscences, Portraits*. New Delhi: Kali for Women, 2001.

Taseer, Aatish, trans. *Manto: Short Stories*. Noida: Random House, 2008.

Zaheer, Sajjad. *The Light: A History of the Movement for Progressive Literature in the Indo-Pak Subcontinent*. A translation of *Roshnai* by Amina Azfar. Karachi: Oxford University Press, 2006.

JOURNALS

Journal of South Asian Literature 20, no. 2, The Writings of Saadat Hasan Manto (Summer/Fall 1985).
Annual of Urdu Studies 16 (2001).

Urdu

BOOKS

Ashk, Upendranath. *Manto: Mera Dushman*. Allahabad: Naya Idarah, 1979.

Bukhari, Ali Sana. *Saadat Hasan Manto (Tehqiq)*. Lahore: Manto
  Academy, 2006.

Chander, Krishan. *Naye Adab Ke Maimar—Saadat Hasan Manto*.
  Bombay: Kutub Publishers, 1948.

Jalal, Ayesha, and Nusrat Jalal, eds. *Manto*. Lahore: Sang-e-Meel
  Publications, 2012.

Manto, Saadat Hasan. *Manto Dramay*. Lahore: Sang-e-Meel, 1996.

———. *Manto Kahanian*. Lahore: Sang-e-Meel, 1995.

———. *Manto Nama*. Lahore: Sang-e-Meel, 1990.

———. *Manto Numa*. Lahore: Sang-e-Meel, 1991.

———. *Manto Rama*. Lahore: Sang-e-Meel, 1990.

Qasimi, Ahmad Nadeem, comp. *Manto ke Khutut, Nadeem Ke
  Naam*. Lahore: Pakistan Books and Literary Sounds, 1991.

Qureshi, Abu Saeed. *Manto (Swaneh)*. Lahore: Idara-i-Faroogh-i-
  Urdu, ca. 1955.

Saeed, Mohammad, ed. *Nau Adarat Manto*. Lahore: Idara-i-
  Faroogh-i-Mutala, 2009.

JOURNALS

Naqoosh—Manto Number. Lahore: Idara-i-Faroogh-i-Urdu, 1955.

Naqoosh—Lahore Number Edited by Mohammad Tufail. Lahore:
  Idara-i-Faroogh-i-Urdu. No. 92 (February 1962), pt. 2.

Index

Index

Index

Index

Manto, Saadat Hasan *(continued)*
  elder brothers of, 30, 32, 60;
  extended family in Lahore, 176;
  father of, 28, 29, 30, 31, 32, 33, 34,
  37, 45, 50; mother of, 28, 29–32,
  33, 46–47, 52, 55–56, 57, 60, 69;
  and Nasira Iqbal (sister), 30, 33,
  46–49, 52, 60–61, 175, 178; and
  Nighat (daughter), 119–120, 123;
  as prankster, ix, 33; relationship
  with children, 178–179; and Safia
  (wife), 60–62, 66–67, 68, 70, 107,
  119, 176; and Safia's family, 69; as
  slacker and gambler, 33; as unworthy son, 33
—ideas, attitudes, themes: American hubris, 195; anticolonialism,
  ix, 34, 36, 58, 64–65, 76, 125–126;
  ashraf society, 163; atom bomb,
  119, 196–197, 198, 203; Bombay,
  55, 113, 119, 134; British authorities, ix, 1, 65–66, 74–76, 126;
  capital punishment, 37–38, 145;
  civic nationalism, 58; colonial
  servitude, 129; communism, 197,
  198, 200, 201, 204; Communist
  Party, 172; as conscientious objector, 179; as contrarian, 33; cosmopolitanism, 26, 27, 89, 91, 227;
  and cricket, 208; criminals, 3, 26,
  57, 105, 106, 113, 225; criticism of
  government, 146–147; death, 51,
  192–193; displaced humanity, x, 3;
  education, 183; Elizabeth Taylor,
  198, 200; emotions, 182; empathy,
  73, 206, 224; ethics, 24; film stars,
  89–90, 92; freedom of expression,
  62, 162–163; friendship, 14, 19–

20, 223 *(see also under* relation-
  ships); Gandhi, 74; Gandhian
  nonviolence, 76; Hindu-Muslim
  tensions and violence, 56–59, 65,
  113, 118–119, 125, 126, 128–129;
  Hindu-Muslim unity, 68; Hollywood, 36, 201; humanism, 78,
  188, 223, 227; humanity, 14, 24,
  26, 58, 78, 113, 125–126, 133, 136,
  141, 145, 156–157, 161, 171; human
  psychology, x, 3, 24, 89, 105–106,
  148–149, 217–218, 225–226;
  hypocrisy, 15, 26, 59, 76, 113, 188,
  209, 218; independence, 65, 119,
  147–148, 180, 190; India, 57–58,
  77, 188, 205; India and Pakistan,
  204–206, 223–224; Indian constitution (1919), 65–66; Indian
  National Congress, 34, 65, 112–
  113, 119, 125; India vs. Pakistan as
  homeland, 129; the ineffable, 53;
  irony, 26–27; Islam, 21, 173, 180–
  181, 182, 202; Islam and jihad,
  220; Jallianwalla Bagh massacre,
  12–13, 42–44, 74, 75, 76; Jinnah,
  89, 181–182; journalists, 104–105;
  Kashmir, 27, 176, 202–204, 224;
  killing/murder, 57, 80–81, 141,
  144, 152; kite flying, 32–33; labor
  and capital, 94, 99; literary iconoclasm, 226; literature, 163, 168–
  169, 173; literature after partition,
  146; love, 105; loyalty to India,
  224; marriage, 62; martyrdom, 15,
  76, 218, 220–221, 222; and mob
  tyranny, 125; modern authors,
  168–169; morality, 52, 57, 58–59,
  89, 217; mosque-temple issue, 68;

256

mothers, 77–78; mullahs, 197; Muslim League, 34, 119; nationalism, 58, 65, 76, 125, 126; obscenity charge, 71, 109, 156–157, 160, 183, 217–218; observation, 23, 63, 66; occult, 33; pacifism, 188, 223; Pakistan, 77, 148, 202; Pakistan and Turkey, 184; Pakistan and United States, ix, 14, 184, 189–192, 194–198, 200–205, 222–223; Pakistan as religious state, 146; Pakistani films and literature, 180; Pakistani state, 172–174; Pakistan's ruling elite, 223; partition, x, 1–2, 3, 19, 23–24, 74, 78–79, 85–86, 133, 137, 141–145, 149–150, 179–180, 190, 205, 224; peace, 206, 227; and photography, 33; pimps, 26, 74, 100, 101, 113; pity of partition, 109, 129, 137; plea for mercy, 32, 33; political leaders, 58, 112–113, 118, 119; poor people, 24, 52, 113, 188–189, 191, 197, 198, 200, 220, 221; postcolonial moment, 151–186; postcolonial Pakistan, 148; prejudice, 209; progress, 168, 169; progressive writers, 163–170, 172–175, 179, 189, 212; prostitutes, x, 26, 52, 58, 68, 71, 75, 76, 94, 100, 101, 102, 106, 113, 225; and realism, 100, 149; religion, 3, 15, 57, 58, 91, 112–113, 126, 129, 137, 142, 188, 209, 213, 218, 225, 226; revolution, 34, 36, 41, 45–46, 51–52, 53–54, 64, 94, 124, 164; sexuality, x, 26, 52–53, 115–116, 160, 193; shoes, 56, 116; socialism, 94; society, 24, 26, 76–77, 105, 106, 149, 169,

184, 217, 218, 225; Soviet Union, 172, 187–188, 197, 198, 200; storytelling, 46, 71; suicide, 53, 70; transnationalism, 26, 54, 64, 68; United States, 187–188, 224; United States and India, 197, 198; United States and Pakistan, 15; United States and Soviet Union, 203; universalist aspirations, 26; violence, 24, 57, 77, 78, 85–86, 128–129, 130, 133, 141–145, 148, 224, 225; Western culture, 96; women, 60, 62, 74, 76, 77–78, 80, 107, 141, 142–144, 148, 169, 225
—literary influences, 3, 26, 27–28, 40, 45, 62–63, 218; Mirza Asadullah Khan Ghalib, xv, 62–63, 70, 210, 215; Maxim Gorky, 40, 50; O. Henry, 26; Victor Hugo, 26, 38, 39–40, 50; D. H. Lawrence, 26; Somerset Maugham, 26; Guy de Maupassant, 26, 45, 218; Jean-Jacques Rousseau, 26; Russian, French, and Chinese literature, 91; Evelyn Waugh, 191–192
—mental state: and blacklisting, 170–171; and career challenges, 69–70; emotional torment of, 48–49, 53, 64, 108; and life in Pakistan, 133, 152, 176, 193; at Mayo Hospital, 192; and mother's death, 69; rumored to be insane, 177; and sister's marriage, 47
—personality and character, 24, 32–33, 47, 56, 58–59, 62, 69, 70, 100, 102–103, 109, 110; barbed tongue of, 104; cleanliness of, 99; confidence of, 106;

Index